Ten Things NOT to Say to Your Gifted Child:

One Family's Perspective

D1051778

Nancy N. Heilbronner
Jennifer Heilbronner Muñoz
Sarah Heilbronner
Joshua Heilbronner

Great Potential Press

Ten Things NOT to Say to Your Gifted Child: One Family's Perspective

Edited by: Jennifer Ault
Interior design: The Printed Page
Cover design: Hutchison-Frey

Published by Great Potential Press, Inc.
7025 E. 1st Avenue, Suite 5
Scottsdale, AZ 85251

Printed and bound in the United States of America using partially recycled paper.

Great Potential Press and associated logos are trademarks and/or registered trademarks of Great Potential Press, Inc.

15 14 13 12 11   5 4 3 2 1

At the time of this book's publication, all facts and figures cited are the most current available. All telephone numbers, addresses, and website URLs are accurate and active; all publications, organizations, websites, and other resources exist as described in this book; and all have been verified as of the time this book went to press. The author(s) and Great Potential Press make no warranty or guarantee concerning the information and materials given out by organizations or content found at websites, and we are not responsible for any changes that occur after this book's publication. If you find an error or believe that a resource listed here is not as described, please contact Great Potential Press.

Library of Congress Cataloging-in-Publication Data

Ten things NOT to say to your gifted child: one family's perspective / Nancy N. Heilbronner ... et al.
   p. cm.
 Includes bibliographical references and index.
 ISBN-13: 978-1-935067-03-0
 ISBN-10: 1-935067-03-6
1. Gifted children--Education--United States. 2. Gifted children--Family relationships--United States. 3. Gifted children--United States--Psychology. I. Heilbronner, Nancy N.
 LC3993.9.T49 2011
 305.9'089083--dc23
        2011017249

Contents

List of Tables and Figures

Acknowledgments

My sincere thanks go to my editors, Jim Webb, Janet Gore, Anne Gore, and Jen Ault, for their support for this work. Many thanks also go to friends and colleagues such as Sally, Joe, Rachel, and Karrie, who all believe in me. Love and thanks go out to my extended family, especially J.R. and Charlie, for always being there. I owe a debt of love and gratitude to my talented adult children, who are the co-authors of this book; I've probably learned more from them than they have from me. Finally, thank you to the unsung hero in all of this, my husband, Fred, who provided me with all the love and encouragement (and coffee) I needed to make it through (which turned out to be gaggles and gaggles of herds and herds…).

Preface

When I was a little girl, I knew that I was somehow different from other children. I craved books, but there weren't many books in my family's home. This didn't dampen my desire to read, though. In fact, the public library was one of the first places I drove to after getting my driver's license. I also knew as a child that I was imaginative and loved to spend long hours daydreaming, but a consequence of that imagination was that I could dream up "what-if" scenarios that seemed real to me—real enough to frighten and confuse me. *What if I flunked the Spanish test? What if the headaches I had were the result of an illness?* And unlike many children, I knew that I could be happy with one or two friends. I knew that I was different, and my parents were often frustrated with these differences.

Don't get me wrong—I was raised in a loving home with caring parents. But in those days, especially in the South, not many people understood the idea of being "gifted," much less how emotionally intense gifted children can be. I think it was through the intensity of my experiences that this book ultimately came into being.

When I saw my own children develop some of these same intensities, I was able to see the issues through the eyes of both a parent and as a gifted individual myself. My professional training as a teacher of the gifted and as a researcher further developed my understanding of the social and emotional needs of gifted children. However, when I reviewed the books that had been published on the topic, I discovered that there was a need for a text that would provide a readable overview of gifted children's social-emotional issues, as well as a book that would give rise to the voices of the children themselves. Then it hit me. Why not write a book describing the issues in a sort of "Top 10" format and include the perspectives of my three adult children? True, they aren't children anymore, but they are not so remotely removed from childhood that they can't remember. Their voices add a different perspective to this book and reinforce the idea that most gifted children turn out well, despite the mistakes that we sometimes make as parents.

Deciding which issues to address in the book was no easy feat. Some of the chapters developed because they were difficult issues in our family (e.g., the chapter on anxieties and fears), and others were included because they are concerns for a large number of gifted parents and children. Reading this book will enable you to understand many of the social-emotional issues that gifted children face, but it's important to remember that, overall, gifted children do not face any *more* social-emotional issues than other children.[1] However, when they do struggle, it tends to be with one of the issues described in this book.

Writing this book has been a labor of love for our family. We laughed and cried as we remembered each story. We told some of the stories with hesitation—some are personal and intense. We did this in the hope that our stories will help other families who have struggled with some of the same issues. We have nicknamed this book "our family therapy."

I'm a big believer in gentle course corrections. We discuss in the book how parenting is like canoeing down a river, and if you've ever canoed, you know that gentle course corrections are better and easier to make than large course corrections. As a parent, you need to listen to and watch your children so that you can make gentle course corrections. You need to understand what the experts say about the issues, but in the end, good parenting has to be based on your own knowledge of your child and the course you're charting together with him or her.

Enjoy the book. But more importantly, enjoy the journey of parenting gifted children. It's a wonderful—and sometimes wild—ride!

Introduction

Alice asks, "Would you tell me, please, which way I ought to go from here?"

"That depends a good deal on where you want to get to," said the Cat.

~Lewis Carroll's *Alice in Wonderland*

Where's the Instruction Manual?

I remember the first night that my husband, Fred, and I spent alone with our infant daughter, Jen. My mom had recently left after spending a generous five days with us. An expert at child-rearing, having raised six children of her own, she made everything look easy, and she'd left us thinking, "How hard could this be?" Now, as we carried our new baby, walking around and around the bedroom in hopes that this would quiet the ear-piercing, shrieking sounds that erupted from her tiny mouth, Fred turned to me in frustration and asked above the wailing, "What's wrong with her?" "I don't know!" I snapped back, my tone of voice revealing the exhaustion I felt in every nerve of my body. "They don't come with instruction manuals!"

Fast forward 25 years. Not only had my husband and I survived that first rough night as parents on our own, we'd gone on to have two more children—Sarah and Josh. Raising a family of three proved to be a challenge, but we did it. Now, as empty-nesters, we were watching *Supernanny*, a television show in which a nanny is called in to help parents of misbehaving, difficult children. I stared in horror as one little boy threw a tantrum and kicked his mother. The mother just sat there. "Why doesn't she take that little boy in hand and teach him not to do that?" I asked. Fred smiled at me, relishing what he was about to say. "Because," he replied, "they don't come with instruction manuals." I think he'd been waiting a long time to say that.

Parenting is a marvelous journey full of unexpected challenges and joys, precisely because there are no instruction manuals. Much of it you learn from experience, and some comes from instinct, which makes for a great adventure. That first night that Fred and I were alone with Jen proved to be a pivotal point in our parenting. After she had been shrieking for more than five hours, we were totally exhausted, and so we did the only thing we could—we gave up and followed our instincts. Carefully, we laid her on the bed face-down (which you're not supposed to do today, but then…who knew?) and began patting her bottom rhythmically. The shrieks became softer, but we were too tired to notice. We were half-asleep, taking turns patting her bottom for about an hour when the crying stopped. Just stopped. Fred and I were startled by the total silence and looked at each other hopefully. Could it really be that we had successfully managed to soothe our daughter to sleep? Sure, it had taken six hours, but in the end, we had been successful. I remember smiling as I lay down, somehow sensing that it would all be okay, even if it would be tough. We were going to be good parents if we followed our instincts because we had good instincts.

Rapids Ahead

In a way, parenting is like a canoe trip down a beautiful river. Anyone who's ever been canoeing will tell you that although there is some basic training for being on the water that must take place, much of the technique you learn from experience, and you need to trust your instincts. You learn how to navigate in calm water, but you also must learn how to recognize rapids and steer clear of them or negotiate them with care. With gifted children, I believe this is especially true. Parenting gifted children is a little like canoeing a difficult river—the one with all of the white-water—before you've had time to practice. You never signed up for it, didn't expect it, and certainly didn't train for it.

Maybe you, the reader, have only recently discovered that you are on a complex and difficult river, but you were suspicious from the start that this wasn't the course most of your friends were on. This river appears to have more unexpected twists and turns and also some amazing opportunities for fun and adventure, but it definitely isn't your "normal" river.

At least, that's the way I felt when I discovered that my children were gifted. As I navigated my own gifted parenting waters, I felt simultaneously relieved and worried—relieved because at last I had a name for why my children were different from other children, but worried because of all that the name implied. What was this thing called "gifted"? Was it real, or was it some label made up for parents of children who just don't quite fit in?

I had many questions—so many, in fact, that I ended up pursuing a Master's degree and ultimately a Ph.D. in gifted education, all inspired by my need to better understand my own children. The journey has been an amazing one, and along the way, I've picked up a few tips. In fact, the journey has now led me to write this book because I realized recently (as I was remembering Fred's comment during the *Supernanny* episode) that although there are guidebooks for parenting gifted children, there are no guidebooks *that include the gifted child's perspective*. I had plenty to say about being a parent in a family with gifted children, but my children had their perspectives, too. Consequently, I have asked that each one of them add their memories, stories, and comments to my own. The purpose of the book is to offer one family's perspective, because I remember all too well what it's like to see your child experience something but have no other experience with which to compare it.

Your Canoeing Guide

The book is organized into 10 chapters. You can read the chapters in any order, but each chapter stands alone. They all offer tips that will guide you in parenting your gifted child, and they're not just my opinion; they're all grounded in decades of research, and while you can look up the research and read it for yourself, this book will also provide you with practical suggestions. Each chapter deals with a particular social-emotional or academic issue relating to giftedness, and for each issue, I have asked one of my children to provide comments in the form of an afterword. Even though they're all adults now, they have written a few pages to tell you what it was like to grow up as a gifted child dealing with these issues. Hopefully, they'll reaffirm the main idea of the book, which is that the important thing isn't to be the perfect parent; it's to have a general understanding of the issues involved with parenting gifted children and how to turn potentially bad situations into good ones. I believe that my children's comments may very well be the most important part of the chapters because they offer a unique perspective of what it's like to be a gifted child living and dealing with some of these issues.

How often do we as parents get to hear the voices of our gifted children, all grown up, discussing the past, their childhoods? Perhaps you will one day, but for now, sit back and imagine your own children in 10 or 20 years. What will they be saying?

I'll be sharing my ideas in a sort of "Top 10" framework because it helps to organize the topics. Thus, I'll be discussing 10 things not to say to gifted children. The "10 things" were developed through research on some of the most common concerns of parents and teachers of gifted children. However, it is with a little trepidation that I present the material this way because I fear that readers might be misguided in two ways: (1) you may believe that the list is presented in some order of importance, and (2) you may think that if you say any of these things to your children, they will never recover. Neither of these ideas is true. Think of each of the 10 things as standing independently of the others, with no "thing" more important than any other "thing." Also, please be assured that saying these things will not permanently ruin your relationship with your child. Most parents have said these things to their children from time to time. I confess, *I've* said these things to *my* children. In spite of my mistakes, I believe that all three turned out okay, but you'll be able to judge that for yourself.

Three Principles

Before I delve into the 10 things not to say to your gifted child, I want to introduce three very important overall parenting principles, which will guide you along the gifted parents' "river" and the "rapids" that may lie ahead. If you take nothing more away from this book, these three principles will help guide you on your parenting path:

1. *Surround your child with unconditional love and a secure environment.*
2. *Respect the uniqueness that is within each child.*
3. *Identify and nurture your child's talents.*

Principle 1. Surround your child with unconditional love and a secure environment

Researchers, such as the psychologist Abraham Maslow,[2] have concluded that children (and adults, for that matter) have a hierarchy of needs that can be visualized as a pyramid (see Figure 1). At the bottom of the pyramid are basic physiological needs, such as food, water, shelter, and clothing. Once these needs are met, we can address the need for safety and then other higher-level needs, such as socialization, self-esteem, and self-actualization, or the need to create and learn at a high level. The base of the pyramid therefore represents fundamental human needs that must be met before other needs are addressed, which makes sense. Your child must have his physical and safety needs cared for before you worry about him making friends. Security means, first and foremost, meeting your child's physical needs. Once these are met, however, you can begin to concentrate on higher levels of needs, including socialization (or belonging), self-esteem needs that come from recognition from others, and self-actualization, or realizing one's potential. To do so, however, your child must feel secure, safe from threat, and loved.

For decades, researchers[3] have noted the importance of the early relationship between mother and infant, a relationship that developmental psychologists refer to as attachment. It is through the security of this loving relationship that children feel safe and are able to go out and explore the world. In gifted children, the love associated with this period of attachment has been linked to the development of empathy and compassion for others.[4] Attachment has also been linked with greater curiosity,[5] increased persistence,[6] and positive attitudes.[7] It's important to consider that money or what a parent can buy are not the most important things—parents at all income levels can provide the type of loving relationship that enables a child to feel secure. It is fairly well-documented and accepted that loving environments are important for all children, but they may be especially important for developing the potential of a gifted child.

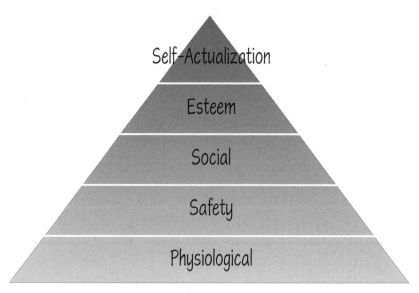

Figure 1. Maslow's Hierarchy of Needs[8]

Principle 2. Respect the uniqueness that is within each child

Besides providing a loving environment, it is important that you respect your child as a unique individual. I like to compare young children to unwrapped birthday presents. Their traits are hidden, wrapped inside their small bodies. It's hard to imagine what they'll grow to be, but grow they will, and the path of their growth will be determined by their own unique combination of genetics and the environment around them.

Scientists have debated *nature vs. nurture* for hundreds of years to try to determine whether environmental influences shape what we become or if we are born that way, and although they have no definite answer yet, it has been determined that we are most likely a product of both nature and nurture—that is, both genetics and environment play a role in who we become. Many babies express early personality traits if you look for them. Some infants coo or laugh while Mom or Dad cooks dinner; others demand to be held constantly. Some are risk takers; others hang back and study situations before attempting any new tasks. These differences are small indicators as to the child's personality. Your child was born with certain innate traits, and the combination of these traits is unique to each child. This unique combination of traits is played out in a unique environment—your child's physical and emotional environment—to shape her into the adult that she will become.

As parents, we should respect that uniqueness and accept that our children will never be us. They will never share all of our likes, dislikes, interests, talents, physical or mental traits, joys, or fears. They will be distinctively themselves, with their own personalities, strengths, and weaknesses. It is through this understanding that we develop some of our best parenting strategies. Expecting children to react the way that we react is setting up a recipe for parenting disaster because we think that what works for us will work for them. We like chess, so they should like chess as much as we do. We became doctors, so they should become doctors. We love music, so they should love music, too. Instead of trying to make our children into miniature versions of ourselves, we need to help them discover who they are as unique individuals and how to live a successful life as themselves.

Principle 3. Identify and nurture your child's talents

The third guiding principle for parenting involves helping your child by identifying and nurturing his talents. Those talents may be in math, science, language, the arts, or more than one of these. He may even have talents across many areas. Most gifted children are by nature highly inquisitive, and they usually want to learn, but there may be complicating factors. Sometimes these bright and eager children want to learn only what *they* want to learn—only what interests them. Sometimes they want to learn but are so bored in school that they end up turn off to learning altogether, becoming acknowledged (or unacknowledged) underachievers. Parents can play a role in turning these types of situations around by understanding their children's interests and using those interests to ignite a passion for learning. Parents can also guide their children so that they understand their own strengths and weaknesses. Parents who do these things can often turn their children into lifelong learners—both academic and creative explorers.

Research and Resources

I'll be discussing many ideas throughout this book, and so I've included two methods for clarification within it: (1) there are endnotes sprinkled throughout the chapters which relate to the References section, and (2) there is an extensive list of resources in the appendix of this book to help you explore each of the ideas further. Although my children and I provide personal anecdotes to illustrate points in each chapter, the research on which the chapters are based is important, and if you wish to delve deeper, you can read these books and articles by some of the leaders in the field of gifted education. The appendix is more "user friendly." Here, you'll find many helpful books, articles, websites, video suggestions, and more that relate to each of the topics that I'll discuss. As an example, the resources provided for this introduction all relate to the characteristics and identification of gifted children.

Afterword by Jen

Hi there. I'm Jen, the daughter from the story about the baby who wouldn't stop crying. I'm more likely to express myself in coherent sentences now, as an adult, but my mother is right—my personality is largely the same today as it was then. From what my parents have told me about my early years, my story wasn't that unusual—I was simply an anxious kid. Although I've learned to manage stress a lot better now, I have not become a totally carefree adult. I was really fortunate, though, to have parents who understood this about me and helped me learn some of the coping mechanisms that have made me a much happier person. It wasn't always smooth or easy. As Mom admitted, both she and Dad said all of these "Top 10" things that they weren't supposed to say more than once and usually out of both love and frustration, but in the end, they found a way to help me to become a better version of myself rather than pushing me to become someone completely different.

It wasn't just me, though. Mom asked each of us to write our notes at the end of her chapters because they did say all of these things to us at one time or another, but I don't think they said *all* of them to any *one* of us. That's because, as obvious as it sounds, we are three different people. We did grow up together in the same family, so we're pretty similar in a lot of ways, but we each presented our parents with our own unique challenges. There were plenty of times they tried something on Sarah or Josh that had worked for me but found that it failed with my two siblings miserably. So whereas I'll respond to the chapter on gifted children's fears, for example, my brother and sister will have their own stories to relate in other chapters.

Sarah, whose reasoning style made us all think she'd grow up to be a lawyer, will tell you some of her tales about the relationship between interest and ability. Josh, who somehow managed to be the only one in our family who can carry a tune, will add his notes to the chapter on creativity. They're both pretty handy with a computer keyboard, so I'll let them introduce themselves.

Mom asked me to write in this section about growing up gifted in our family. I will start with something she hasn't mentioned. Her learning about giftedness wasn't only about finding a label for the three of us. When she says that gifted children "just don't quite fit in," she isn't just talking about her children (or yours, for that matter). Both of my parents were gifted children themselves, although the labels didn't work quite the same way back then. It was when I became a teenager that I realized that my parents sometimes didn't quite fit in either.

Yes, Sarah, Josh, and I grew up in a home with two gifted adults. I mention this because it really shaped our family life and our childhood in many ways, just a few of which I'll share here. Our parents identified with us as we struggled with the issues that are exaggerated in gifted children, sometimes with funny or touching results.

Mom and Dad set up an extremely intellectual home that meshed well with our need for stimulation and challenge. Before they moved a few years ago, for instance, they donated many boxes of books to a local library, but the movers still rolled their eyes when it came time to pack the remaining library into the truck. My parents' house has always overflowed with books. (Unfortunately, I inherited this decorating style and found, sadly, that it is better suited to a suburban house than to a Boston apartment, but I can't seem to part with the books.) I'd like to say that these books were all high-brow literature, but in fact, the collection was eclectic—a glut of miscellaneous information about any subject that had ever struck my parents as interesting. Trashy mysteries were crammed in next to old travel guides, Shakespearean plays, and the newest paperbacks. We occasionally tried to organize them but to no avail. There was no system to their placement on the shelves (and tables and floors). This would drive me crazy now, but for a kid, it was actually pretty great. Mom and Dad rarely forbade us to read anything we found there, and the lack of organization kept me from permanently pigeonholing myself into a particular genre. I'd go to the bookshelf looking for another fantasy novel, or whatever, and before I found one, I'd find some historical fiction book that caught my attention. I received a fairly broad exposure to many subjects from those bookshelves.

Lest you think this was purely a solo activity, I should mention that my mother's encyclopedias, now 40 years old, often played a pivotal role at our dinner table conversations. We would be talking about the Sahara, salmonella, or the Senate, and eventually one of us would shout, "Get the S encyclopedia!" (Somehow it always seemed to be S.) Josh, as the youngest, was dispatched to the office to retrieve it, and he came trudging back with the volume that enlightened us on the geography of Suriname, the history of the screwdriver, or the various types of squash. I could go on. Adam Smith? South Dakota? Classes of ships? You get the point. As young children, we learned to ask questions but also to look for answers. And yes, one of us was always assigned to do the literal looking.

Our vacations played out pretty much the same way. We lived in South Florida, so we did go to Disney World in Orlando, but the trips we remember best were the educational treks that had the feel of a *National Lampoon's Vacation* movie. Our parents bought a camp trailer and drove us around the country, stopping to enjoy all sorts of historical sites and geological oddities. I won't claim that we were always perfect travelers, but we did develop a taste for this sort of exploration. Just recently, Mom says that Sarah and I intentionally tried to make her hair go gray during two recent summers we spent in places that worried her (Israel and Russia). Actually, we were just doing what she and my dad had taught us to do—visit places that interested us.

This may be the best way to end this introduction. Like most children, I've done things that have amused, frightened, and confused my parents. We have had many conversations—some of them contentious—about everything from my decision to quit piano lessons to my impractical choice of a college major. In each case, though, my parents followed their instincts and gave the three of us the support and confidence we needed to go where we wanted to go, do what we needed to do, and be who we needed to be. Of course they also gave us the help we needed to figure all those things out in the first place. We were pretty lucky. Since you're asking some questions that led you to open this book, I'm betting your children will be just as lucky.

CHAPTER 1

You're So Smart... We Love You!

The Problem with Equating Being Smart with Being Loved

Once we believe in ourselves, we can risk curiosity, wonder, spontaneous delight or any experience that reveals the human spirit.

~e.e. cummings

I was sitting in the car with my daughter, Sarah, after attending her high school awards ceremony. She had just won the school-wide science award, but she was crying.

"Mom, I don't deserve this award," she sobbed. "I'm a fraud, and I don't deserve this award."

I was stunned. Winning awards was not unusual for my daughter. An overachiever, this was a child who never received less than an A on a report card and whose teachers remarked, "I wish I had 30 more like her." As early as kindergarten, she'd been doing her homework without being asked. Her focus was on performance, always wanting the high score and always trying to prove herself, not only through grades, but also through demanding extracurricular activities such as piano, band, scouts, Red Cross, and volunteer work. She was driven to achieve the best and to be the best. She was class valedictorian, and when it came time to select a college, she applied early-decision to the one college she felt was the best for her.

"Where have you decided to apply?" I asked one day as I noticed her filling out an application.

"Well," she answered matter-of-factly, "I'm applying early-admission to Harvard, and then after that we'll see."

"Really," I responded, "Harvard's extremely difficult to get into. Do you think you should line up some other schools?"

"I will," was her response, "if I need to."

There was no need. She was accepted into Harvard via the early-admission process. My child's dedication had evidently paid off. And now, *after* learning of her acceptance into Harvard, we were sitting in our car at night in the high school parking lot, and Sarah was crying. She had just won the science award for the school. Sitting by her side in the auditorium as her name was called, I saw the look on her face, and it was a look of astonishment. She was shocked. I literally had to prod her to rise to accept the award. She was shaking and white as she came back and took her place by my side, award in hand.

But now my child was in tears. "I don't deserve this award," she whispered. "I'm a fraud, and I don't deserve this award."

"Of course you deserve the award," I replied. "You've never gotten less than an A in science, and you won the regional science fair."

"No, Mom, you don't understand, "she responded in a jittery voice. "There are kids in my class…boys…who understand it so much better. They deserve it, not me. And if I don't deserve this, maybe I don't deserve to go to Harvard."

I was bewildered. Here was a child who could not see herself as the rest of the world saw her—a competent achiever. As we talked, I learned that she saw herself as an imposter and feared the loss of the world's approval. She thought, incorrectly, that if she didn't achieve at the highest level, she was a failure and that others wouldn't like her or respect her any more. Her identity and self-worth were too tied up in her ability to achieve awards and accolades.

This was not a new concern with Sarah, but I had never seen it manifest in such extreme form. Through the years, a pattern had emerged that our family actually teased her about. It usually started with Sarah announcing an upcoming challenge—a major test, a speech, or maybe a recital. She would dutifully prepare for the challenge, working diligently for days, weeks, or sometimes even months. As the day of the challenge drew near, she would declare her lack of preparedness, despite the fact that we all knew she was well prepared. The day would come, she would meet the challenge (usually well), and we would sit back because we knew what was coming next. Sarah would cry, having convinced herself that she did poorly We would all comfort her and use gentle humor to try to bring her out of this phase, which usually served to soothe her for a while. If the challenge took the form of a test, she would bring home the A nonchalantly a few days later, often without telling us. A few weeks later, we might be sitting around the dinner table and remember the test. We'd ask her, "So did you get your test grade back?" She would reply, "Yes, it was an A. I think it was the highest grade in the class." We would look at her incredulously, having trouble believing that this was the same child who had been in tears the week before. It didn't matter—she had moved on to worrying about the next challenge.

The Pitfalls of Equating Self-Worth with Achievement

Many gifted children are overachievers and, like Sarah, are driven to perfection. But sometimes a child's sense of worth is too closely tied to achievement. Of course, we all love our children and are proud of them, and so it is only natural to want to praise them to the high heavens. It's especially difficult for parents of gifted achievers to avoid praising them for being smart, especially when the awards and accolades are all about being smart or talented or gifted. But here's the problem: The more emphasis we as parents place on these awards and achievements, the more our children may come to rely on these same accolades for their own feelings of self-worth. They may see our approval and think, if only subconsciously, "I need to keep this up—it's what I am. I'm smart and talented, and that's why people love me. And if I stop being smart, they probably won't love me."

As parents, it's never our intention to convey this message, and so we may be baffled when we see our children striving beyond our expectations to achieve perfection in grades and scores. We may view their tears with puzzlement as they cry over a B on a test. However, we need to be honest in understanding how they arrived at that moment. Sometimes over-praise, or constantly rewarding achievement with praise, can lead to a child equating self-worth with how well we do what we do. Our view of ourselves as competent or not competent is influenced by what researchers call self-efficacy, which is the belief in our ability to perform well at specific tasks within a field or domain.[9] For example, if you say that you're good in math, you're demonstrating your belief that you are capable of performing well in math. You have high self-efficacy in math. It is possible to have high self-efficacy in one field and low self-efficacy in another. If you believe that you can solve advanced mathematics problems but cannot write well, you demonstrate high self-efficacy in math but low self-efficacy in writing.

Self-efficacy is different from self-confidence, for self-confidence has to do with an overall feeling about how you deal with life. If you are a self-confident person, you probably believe that you are fairly capable overall and face challenges with confidence. Self-efficacy, on the other hand, is more specific and pertains to skills required to complete tasks within a field or domain. For example, the domain of science requires certain types of skills such as critical and analytical thinking, as well as some memorization. If you believe that you are not good at science, you are demonstrating low self-efficacy in science. What you are really saying, though, is that you do not believe that you can perform the skills required to do well in science. This may or may not be true, depending on how realistically you have appraised your abilities. You may actually be good at those skills, but for a variety of reasons, you believe that you are not. We all have these feelings of being able to perform better in some areas and not as well in others. The problem is not with the feelings themselves; rather, the problem occurs when we equate these feelings of self-efficacy with self-worth

A number of factors influence whether we see ourselves as capable or good at something or not. Researchers[10] have discovered that individuals who believe that abilities may be improved with effort are more likely to persist at difficult tasks. We also know that over time, these individuals learn to be successful at more and more complex tasks, resulting in an increased feeling of competence. Because they view their successes as a result of hard work instead of innate ability, they reason that if they try harder, they will improve. On the other hand, individuals who believe that abilities are innate, fixed, and unchangeable are less likely to persist if a task becomes more difficult, and often they falter. They reason that they are no longer talented or smart at something because it is no longer easy.

Let's look at an example. Suppose you're a fifth-grade student sitting in a classroom and your teacher is about to give back last week's math test, which was on three-digit division. You have been told by your mom and dad that you're very smart in math, and your teacher has lavished praise on you. You fully expect that you will receive a top score on the test, which you do. As a matter of fact, you exceed everyone's expectations because you completed the extra credit, resulting in the best score in the class. "Wow," croons the teacher as she hands back your test paper. "You're really very smart in math. Congratulations! Top score!" You smile outwardly and inwardly, soaking up the warm praise. When you arrive home, your parents proudly display your test paper on the refrigerator. They tell everyone how smart you are in math, and you bask in a warm glow of love and approval.

Fast-forward a couple of months, and you might find that it's getting harder to achieve the top score in math. Your teacher has started covering exponents, and you're having trouble (for the first time) understanding what she's saying. It doesn't occur to you that you have to work harder to prepare for the test on exponents. Why should you? You've never had to work before. You know you're talented. The day of the test comes, and you're not worried because you know you're smart in math. You take the test. A few days later, with a worried look on her face, the teacher hands your test back. Wordlessly, you take it from her and recoil in shock at your score—a D. You look back up into your teacher's face. Is that a look of disappointment? You worry silently what could have happened. After all, you are supposed to be smart in math, aren't you? At least that's what everyone has been telling you, but now you begin to doubt yourself. You feel like an imposter. If doing well on the last math test means that you're smart in math, then doing poorly on this one must mean that you're no good anymore, which maybe you suspected all along.

This example is a condensed version of what often happens to gifted students. The time between success and lack of success in real life in a field of study often isn't measured in weeks, but rather in years. A child may be able to easily complete his work in elementary or middle school but struggle more in high school or college, or even on his first job. Gifted students who do not learn how to work hard in elementary or middle school are often at a disadvantage in high school and college, for it is during the early years that important study skills and work habits are formed. To become good students, children must learn skills such as how to read and reflect on text, organize and manage information, and monitor their own learning. They must learn that hard topics require persistence, a concept that some researchers call *task persistence*.[11] As the work grows harder over time, the child who does not learn these lessons may come to question his ability. A child who believes that he is talented in math in elementary or middle school may come to believe during high school—when he has to work harder to maintain high grades—that he is no longer talented.

Students who approach their studies in this way are also known as a *performance learners* because they focus on performance indicators such as grades, test scores, and other external indications of achievement. If the student doesn't obtain a high (sometimes the highest) score, she is not only disappointed; she may also feel that she has failed. Coupled with this emphasis on performance, she participates in a type of black-and-white thinking—if she does well, she is a success, but if she does poorly, she is a failure, and the stakes are high. If she fails, she may come to believe that she is not talented, not smart, and her self-confidence may plummet.

In the early 1980s, researcher Felice Kaufmann conducted a follow-up study of 172 Presidential Scholars from the years 1964-1968. These individuals had been academically high-achieving students in high school, scoring in the top 1% on the National Merit Scholarship Qualifying Test. They had garnered numerous awards and accolades, and yet in this study, many looked back and wondered if it might have been better to have been praised less for achievement. One participant in the research commented:

> *I expected the achievements and recognition in high school. I had always had them. In college, I had a harder time, more difficulty achieving and no support or recognition. A reaction set in—rejection of all the achievement, a get-by attitude. I do think I would have been better off with a little less recognition. I buckled under the responsibility and pressure to keep up that pace. I was also so diversified that I couldn't find a single channel for my efforts. Result: no career goals and no awards.*[12]

A common theme from the former Presidential Scholars in the Kaufmann study was that many of them experienced loss of self-worth and loss of identity once they stopped getting awards. As adults, they realized that they had defined success as getting awards, and once there were no more awards (after college), they weren't sure how to view themselves. Some of them who had gone on to careers in academia or research had left those areas completely to be farmers or participate in the arts. Their advice to other gifted individuals was to find what interests you, and don't equate success with the number of academic awards you receive. Success can also come from being an organic farmer.

In contrast to performance learners are those students who believe that ability may be improved with effort. These students are more likely to persist when the task becomes difficult.[13] They believe that if they work harder and longer to attain goals, they are more likely to achieve those goals. They do not place as much emphasis on being smart or on performance indicators such as grades and test scores, but instead they view the goal of learning to be the mastery of a task or skill or the accomplishment of a goal, and so consequently they are known as *mastery learners.* Mastery learners view learning as a continuous process. They focus on their short-term and long-term goals, working incrementally to achieve those goals. They are able to celebrate successes and learn from failures, and ever-present is the notion that abilities may be improved through continuous effort—a healthier approach to learning.

Parenting the Overachiever

As parents, we want to encourage our children to acquire the outlook and habits of mastery learners, because if they begin to view their own learning as a continuous process, they will be more likely to persist through short-term difficulties. They will also be less likely to view success and achievement in black-and-white terms, and they will begin to think about learning as a process that can be encouraged and maintained (with effort) over time. They won't be so apt to give up and quit when they find things difficult, and they are less likely to judge themselves as failures if they fail or get less than perfect grades when first learning new skills.

What can parents do to encourage their children to develop into mastery learners? First, we need to talk about what *not* to do. Don't say to your children, "You're so talented (or smart, capable, gifted, brilliant, etc.)." And especially don't equate these traits with approval and love, saying, "We love that you're so smart," which implies, "We love you because you are smart, and by implication, we would love you less if you were not so smart—or so highly achieving."

Perfectionism and Fear of Failure

In some children, the effects of equating achievement with approval may be compounded by perfectionist tendencies. It has long been recognized that many gifted children (although not all) are perfectionists.[14] Researchers have disagreed for years about why some gifted children are at risk for perfectionism, but it may have to do with how they see things. Perhaps they see and focus on the ideal. For example, the gifted artist can see in his mind's eye how he wants his painting to turn out, but actually painting it that way may be more than he can accomplish.

Researchers also disagree as to whether perfectionism is a positive[15] or a negative trait.[16] Some researchers now view perfectionism as existing on a continuum. At one end of the continuum are the "normal" perfectionists, who use their perfectionist tendencies to accomplish high-quality work, but they do not let these tendencies interfere with their daily functioning. They take pleasure and pride in their work. At the other end of the continuum are "neurotic" perfectionists, who feel little or no satisfaction with their work, possibly because they never think that it is good enough. They frequently experience difficulties in coping, may procrastinate, and may experience depression and shame or guilt more frequently than their "normal" perfectionist counterparts.[17]

If you have a child who tends toward troublesome perfectionism, it can be difficult. She may never see that that her work is good, and she may obsess over it endlessly. She may procrastinate starting an assignment, or she may never finish it, often because she sets impossibly high goals for herself. For example, instead of wanting to write a fun short story, she may tell herself that she has to write the next great American novel or nothing at all. It's probably impossible to change her perfectionist tendencies completely, but there are things you can do as a parent to encourage her to move toward the healthy end of the continuum.

Educators[18] suggest that although perfectionistic tendencies may be inborn, they are also frequently nurtured in the child's home and school environment. Generally (and I can vouch for this in my own case), parents of perfectionists promote an atmosphere of excellence, in which achievement is emphasized—not that this is a bad thing, but it is important for parents to be aware of it. There is often pressure, verbalized or not, for the child to succeed. You as a parent must try to understand the nature and the amount of the pressure on your child to do well, both at home and at school. Is it reasonable? Also be aware of perfectionist tendencies in yourself, which your child probably senses, even if you have not discussed it.

The next thing that you can do is to discuss perfectionism with your child—what it means to you and what it means to him. Point out the positives of healthy perfectionism, and tell him that you would like to work with him to develop these traits. Positive perfectionism is when children (and adults) understand deadlines and ideal outcomes and can plan their work to take these into account, but it doesn't derail them from the task at hand. Healthy perfectionists don't become so overwhelmed that they procrastinate excessively or shut down. Help your child to become aware of these differences between healthy and neurotic perfectionism. Let him know that you don't expect him to be perfect all of the time and that you also sometimes struggle with perfectionism (if you do). Point out the times when you did things less than perfectly.

In our family, I also used a "what's the worst thing that could happen" approach with our children, in which I spun a given situation out to its logical conclusion in an effort to help my children understand that even the worst things they could imagine were not so terrible. For example:

Sarah: Mom, I got a C on a test!!!

Mom: That's too bad.

Sarah: Don't you understand? I might get a B in the course now!

Mom: And so what's the worst thing that could happen?

Sarah: I won't have a 4.0 GPA anymore.

Mom: And so what's the worst thing that could happen after that?

Sarah: I won't get into Harvard!

Mom: And so what's the worst thing that could happen after that?

Sarah: Hmmm (puzzled look)…nothing, I guess. I'll get into another college.

Others[19] advocate a similar approach to help children and adults put things into perspective. In this approach, people write down the worst-case scenario and then examine, like a good detective, how likely that scenario is. Next, they write down the best-case outcome and again examine the evidence to determine how likely it is. Finally, they write down the most likely outcome and the evidence for it. Of course, to do this exercise, you don't actually have to write things down; you can simply talk about them in the same way, though writing helps to keep the feelings at arm's length.

Help your child learn to set reasonable goals for herself (e.g., write a short story instead of a book) based on the time and resources at hand. And, to tie back into our ideas on mastery learning, teach that the process itself (rather than the outcome) is important. For example, instead of emphasizing grades and scores, help your child develop a long-term view of learning. Talk with her and let her know that abilities may be improved with effort. Help her to develop an understanding that this improvement takes place over a long period of time. Expose her to biographies of individuals who have mastered their crafts, but who may have taken a lifetime to do so (see some of the resources in the appendix of this book). Babe Ruth, Eleanor Roosevelt, Martin Luther King, Jr., and many more prominent achievers realized that success is the result of a lifetime of effort.

Talk with your child about self-talk.[20] Many children participate in self-talk but may not be aware of the phenomenon. Self-talk consists of the silent conversation that they carry in their heads, and for many high-achieving perfectionists, the practice may be detrimental. Nothing is ever quite good enough for their demanding inner voice. The amazing paper they turn in, the project they work for months on—nothing they do can meet the exacting standards of the inner voice, even when things are good. When things turn bad, it's even worse. They will earn the eventual C on a test, and the inner voice may turn bitter and nasty. "You're no good," the voice may say. The voice may even say, "You're not a good person," which is another issue altogether. These inner voices add to the overall stress level of our children.

The first step to helping a child overcome negative self-talk is to help him become aware of the practice. Asking him to write down his thoughts may help. Have him draw a line down a sheet of paper. On the left size of the page, ask him to write his thoughts. On the right side, have him write facts or counter-arguments to those thoughts. For example, if he writes, "I got a C on a test and so I'm not a good person," on the left, he could counter with, "Just because I got a C, that doesn't make me a bad person. It means I should work to understand why I got the C and maybe work harder to study for the next test," on the right side.

Also, talk with your child about failure. I've often considered how we as parents don't do this, yet failure is a part of life, and we must all learn to deal with it. You might discuss times in your life when you had to overcome failure, or you might expose your child to stories of eminent individuals who struggled from time to time with failure. Because so many things come easily to gifted children, they may not be aware that failure is commonplace and that it may be used as an opportunity to learn how to overcome obstacles. Discuss the failed test, poor performance in the spelling bee, and more. Don't be afraid to have the discussion, and don't emphasize to the child how disappointed you might be. Help your child come to understand that learning is a process that may be improved by effort, and that even "smart" people need to put in this effort to succeed, especially as tasks become harder. Discuss with your child why putting in this effort is worthwhile—that it can lead to a lifetime of satisfaction and happiness if she becomes involved with a career about which she is passionate.

When it comes to praise, use targeted, specific praise. Don't use phrases such as, "Good job!" or "That was brilliant!" Praise specific outcomes, and especially target the praise toward the child's effort. For example, if you know that your middle schooler worked especially hard to qualify for the school's spelling bee and has succeeded, you could say something like, "I can tell that you worked really hard to master that difficult spelling list." This type of praise does two things. First, it targets a specific behavior (i.e., mastering the spelling list) rather than a general characteristic such as "being smart." By targeting a specific behavior, you do not set the child up to think that he's not smart if he doesn't do well in the future. Second, the praise is directed at the student's effort and not at his abilities. Effort is something that he can control, and the statement helps him to internalize the understanding that if he works harder, he is more likely to succeed.

Over time, the impact of using such strategies adds up. The outcome is (hopefully) a child who is kinder and gentler about her own failures. This child will be more likely to persist when the task becomes difficult. This child views learning as a process of developing a set of skills and knowledge that build one upon the other over the course of a lifetime. In short, this child is becoming a mastery learner.

Table 1.1. Parenting Strategies to Develop Mastery Learning in Gifted Children

- ✔ Recognize and discuss perfectionism with your child, including your own.

- ✔ Help your child set reasonable goals.

- ✔ Emphasize process more and product less.

- ✔ Discuss how learning is a continual, long-term process.

- ✔ Discuss how abilities may be improved with effort.

- ✔ Use targeted, specific (rather than general) praise.

- ✔ Discuss the role of failure and how failure may be used to learn how to overcome obstacles.

- ✔ Expose your child to biographies of prominent individuals who have built a lifetime of achievement.

- ✔ Expose your child to biographies of prominent individuals who have dealt with failure.

Afterword by Sarah

I'm a little embarrassed reading the story about bursting into tears following a successful awards ceremony. I wish I could say that I don't overreact that way anymore, but fear of failure still looms large for me, often shaping my actions. Nevertheless, being able to acknowledge the problem with my parents helped reduce the episodes. I can manage them now, and I respond more appropriately to successes and failures. Or so I'd like to think.

My sister and I were both affected at a young age by the need to achieve, and since then, we've met other young women afflicted by the same anxieties we had, so I think it's fairly common. Jen was only months away from leaving to begin college at Yale—by all accounts, a bright future ahead of her—when she confided in me she was scared. Having received only one grade lower than an A in her entire life (in middle school home economics!), she worried that if she lost her identity as the girl with perfect grades, she wouldn't know who she was anymore. This sounds extreme, but for high-achieving students, it is quite common. I felt this acutely when I left for college, too, and when I related the story to my new roommates, they all echoed the sentiment.

Now that I'm in graduate school, I think a lot about the concept of self-efficacy. I see people (especially women) leave challenging scientific careers because they believe that they're not geniuses—unlikely to win the Nobel—so they convince themselves that it's not worthwhile to continue to pursue their dreams. As I write this, I'm on my way to a major neurobiology conference where reactions to my work will likely be mixed. Some people will find it enlightening, but others will voice criticisms. How a scientist deals with criticism seems to me to be a major determining factor for success. Some scientists are able to acknowledge the criticisms, learn from them, and adjust their work accordingly. Others shut down, focusing on the criticisms, believing that flaws make them an inherently bad scientist. Instead of learning from the feedback, they will quit. I have seen differences in self-efficacy play out in precisely this way with many of my colleagues, especially with young women.

In the introduction, Mom made the point that personality and behavior depend on both genetics and experience. That's true, but my professors have taught me that some traits are inherent, which means that someone can be born with a stronger genetic predisposition toward a particular trait, and it will be more difficult to change that trait with experience. I believe that for Jen and me (especially me!), performance learning is an inherited trait.

For both Jen and myself, the story has a happy ending. We both received our first less-than-ideal grades and then...nothing bad happened. We persisted and both found areas in which success meant more than grades. And I know that at the upcoming conference, a harsh critique won't end my scientific career, although my drive for performance will make me upset at the failure.

Our parents never made their love contingent upon performing well. Knowing I had their unconditional love and support gave me the confidence to pursue my passion, even if it meant risking failure.

CHAPTER 2

You're Gifted; This Should Be Easy for You!

Dealing with Underachievement in Gifted Children

I have always grown from my problems and challenges, from the things that don't work out—that's when I've really learned.

~Carol Burnett

Every parent has likely made at least one mistake that he or she regrets. Maybe you lost your temper or said the wrong thing. For me, the parenting moment of which I'm least proud is when I lost control with my son, Josh. Josh is our youngest child, the one who was destined to fulfill several of the stereotypes about youngest children—specifically, that youngest children are easy to care for because we parents are more relaxed, and youngest children are also less motivated because we parents have spent all of our energies motivating their older siblings. Stereotypes are often untrue, but in Josh's case, at least some were true. He has always been very relaxed, even as an infant. Whereas both girls had wailed whenever

I put them down for even a few seconds, Josh was content to be placed in his baby seat with a rattle and a few toys. He'd happily gurgle, watching the play of sunlight across the room while I did household chores. And later, when Josh was older, I noticed that he fulfilled one other stereotype about youngest children—he was far less motivated to achieve.

Josh attended the same school as his sisters, and I expected the same results. His sisters were straight-A students—what some researchers call *school-house gifted*.[21] They couldn't wait to get to school, always did their homework before being asked, and genuinely seemed to enjoy tackling large projects and difficult tests. They were teacher-pleasers. Naturally, we expected the same from Josh. But we noticed differences early, when Josh entered first grade and we had to remind him several times before he would start his homework. His papers were scattered and incomplete. He always did just enough to get by, but never anything extra. These patterns started early, and when he was younger, it wasn't a problem. However, as he entered middle school and the work became more difficult, it became more of an issue. The gap between what we thought he was capable of and what he was actually doing became wider.

Before I discuss this further, you need to understand two things about my son: (1) he is definitely bright, and (2) when motivated, he works extremely hard. We discovered that he was very bright almost by accident, because Josh didn't display the typical behaviors of advanced children, and so we never considered having him evaluated for gifted classes. Then, one day in fourth grade, his teacher approached me and asked, "Why don't you have Josh evaluated for the gifted program?" At that point in time, I was the enrichment coordinator for his school, which meant that I certainly should have been able to recognize students who had potential to qualify for the gifted program. Could I have overlooked my own son?

I had always been reluctant for Josh to be evaluated. Because I was a teacher of the gifted, I understood the conflict that can occur within a family if one child makes it into the gifted program and another doesn't. To make matters worse, the state we lived in

(Florida) required that, to be evaluated for the gifted program, a student had to be recommended by a teacher and then take an IQ test. I'd seen bright, motivated children score a 127 on an IQ test, three points short of the 130 required to be admitted into the program. Many states have now moved away from assessing children using IQ test scores because of the problems associated with using them as the sole means for identification (e.g., the student might not be feeling well on the day of the test, or the test may not measure the child's creative abilities, among other reasons). However, educators in Florida at the time still viewed giftedness as primarily IQ-based.

When Josh took an IQ test, officials in the district invited his father and me to review the results of the assessment. We sat around a table with a child-study team and listened in shock to what they told us. Basically, they told us that Josh was bright—in fact, very bright. He didn't just qualify for the gifted program, he qualified with plenty of room to spare. His father and I sat, stunned, unable to believe what we were hearing. Our son, who had to be reminded to do his homework, our son, who never opened a textbook, our son, who brought home mostly B's and C's, was gifted, and probably highly gifted. What did that mean? I didn't want to think about what it meant for me. I was the gifted teacher, after all, and I certainly should never have missed identifying my own son! What was going on?

This little story illustrates the fact that as parents, we often lose perspective when it comes to our own children. I knew all of the facts about what giftedness could "look" like. I certainly understood that a child didn't have to earn straight A's to be gifted, yet I had overlooked my own son because his school behavior was different from that of my girls.

Josh entered the gifted program in fourth grade and often struggled with deadlines and grades. Sometimes he wanted to drop out, but his father and I encouraged him to persist (see Chapter 9, If It's Too Hard, Then Quit). He remained in the gifted program—a very good gifted program—throughout the remainder of elementary and middle school. When he brought home anything less than a B, we were not happy. Now that we knew how bright he was, we were firmly convinced that we were dealing with some of the issues of underachievement—which brings me to yet another story.

Underachievement

Josh was in ninth grade, and his science project was due. I had asked him about his project repeatedly—when it was first assigned, and again in stages along the way until the very day it was due. Josh reassured me that he had it all under control. "Don't worry, Mom, I'm dealing with it," he would reply. He was able to describe, in vague and general terms, his topic for investigation and his plans for completing the project. I should have known better, but I relaxed and trusted that he would get it done. Then came the phone call. In the story that follows, I have changed the teacher's name to protect the innocent.

When I picked up the call, I recognized the voice of my son's high school science teacher. "Mrs. Heilbronner? This is Mrs. Jackson calling."

"Hello, Mrs. Jackson. What can I do for you today?" I replied, as I cast my eye about for Josh.

"Well, [long pause] I wanted to let you know that…." My attention drifted as I noticed my son motioning frantically to get my attention.

"Mom!" he whispered loudly, "There's something I have to tell you!"

The soft yet firm voice over the phone pulled me back. "…your son's science project has not yet been turned in. It was due last week, and as a matter of fact, his is the only project not yet completed."

I shot a glance over at my son, who was now cowering, watching for my reaction. "Thank you. He'll turn it in tomorrow," I replied, trying to keep my voice even.

Those of you who have watched Bill Cosby have probably seen the skit in which he confronts a misbehaving child. "I brought you into this world," he scoffs, "and I can take you out of it." I have always admired this strategy for dealing with children. Don't get me wrong—I'm not advocating physical punishment. Rather, parents need to be in control, which enables them to provide protective boundaries within which children need to function. My husband and I rarely ever resorted to spanking, but we did believe in letting our children know that we were in charge, which is a good thing… as long as you can control your emotions. What happened next was an example of a rare instance in which I momentarily lost control of my emotions.

"What were you thinking?" I heard my voice rising in pitch. "You told me you had finished that project! Well, you're going to do it now! And you're going to do it by tomorrow!!! This should be easy for you!" Then I pulled my cringing son by the ear—that's right, you read that correctly—by the *ear*, just like parents did a century ago, and I led him out to the car. We raced off to the office supply store to purchase a science project board and some markers. When we returned home, I opened the door to my son's room, escorted him inside, and shut the door behind him. "Stay in there until it's finished!" I shouted. Boy, was I steamed!

Some of you might read this story and think, "What's the big deal? She didn't beat him or threaten him." Others of you might think that I'm the Attila-the-Hun parent. It all depends on your own experiences and perspective, but I'll tell you why I'm not proud of this story. It's one of a very few times when the whole parenting thing got to me—and I handled the situation without reason, with raw emotion only. I knew, even then, that the way I was handling it wouldn't help Josh become a better student or more truthful. The truth was, Josh was scared to tell his father or me about his failings. He knew he was not "school-house gifted" like his sisters and never would be. I suspect he didn't know how to deal with that realization. Reacting the way I did was not the way to help him. I'm glad to report that Josh's story has a happy ending, primarily because of the second trait I mentioned—that he achieves when he is motivated—but I'll save those examples for another chapter. For now, it's enough to understand that gifted students do sometimes underachieve, and there may be many reasons for this fact.

Underachievement is defined as a "discrepancy between the child's school performance and some index of his or her actual ability, such as intelligence, achievement, creativity scores, or observational data."[22] Basically, this means that underachievement is a gap between what a student is capable of doing, measured by some test or other type of assessment, and what he actually does in school. Underachievement in gifted children is tricky because an underachieving gifted child may still be able to keep up with the average work in the class. So underachievement is about achieving less than what the student is capable of achieving.

It may help to think in terms of metaphor, and I like to think of an underachieving gifted student as a fast, sleek car with a problem. Imagine that you own a magnificent red Ferrari capable of reaching speeds of more than 100 mph, yet something prevents the car from going that fast. You take it to a mechanic, where it is diagnosed with a mechanical problem such as a faulty spark plug. You don't hesitate to fix the car, because you know that if the car is fixed, you will be out on the highway going 100 mph, at which point you will be pulled over and fined for speeding. Okay, maybe the metaphor should end there. The point is that you know the car is capable of performing well, and so you do everything you can to fix the problem.

What does underachievement "look" like? Researchers have studied underachievement in gifted children,[23] and although there is no one profile of underachieving students, we do see similar patterns of behavior. Often, underachievement will manifest itself several years after a child enters school, in late elementary or middle school. The child may have been praised in kindergarten, first, or second grade for remarkable performance. Perhaps she read early or performed complex division problems in kindergarten, and she received praise for these abilities. Sometimes the student feels that she cannot keep up with this level of performance and so will start to avoid the behavior so as not to fail and disappoint everyone. As the student grows older, she may start to rebel against authority, lowering her expectations for her own performance. By the end of middle school, parents and teachers are shaking their heads and wondering how such a bright, promising student has slipped to the point of near failure.

What are some of causes for gifted students' underachievement? Returning to the Ferrari metaphor, we may definitely state that gifted children are more complex than cars, and the problem is not always "mechanical"—or, when you're dealing with human beings, the problem often is more than the biological. Of course, some underachievement can be related to biological factors such as poor eyesight or hearing, nutritional issues, hypoglycemia, and more. More frequently, however, there are other factors that place a child at risk for underachievement, and these factors fall into three categories: student factors, family factors, and school-related factors.[24]

Student factors include a host of causes, such as organizational or study skill problems, emotional problems, and learning disabilities. Family factors include temporary issues, such as disruptions caused by a move or a death or illness in the family, and more permanent issues, such as sibling relationships or a chronically ill parent. In Josh's case, we are pretty firmly convinced that attending school in the shadow of his two high-achieving sisters made him feel that he couldn't possibly compete.

School-related factors must also be considered, including the overall school climate. Students are motivated in school when three things occur: (1) when they expect their results to have the desired outcome, (2) when they believe they have the skills to be successful, and (3) when they trust the environment and believe that they will be successful in it.[25]

When considering the school environment, an informed parent will ask several questions. First, is there a respect for the child and for learning in the school? In the classroom? Next, underachieving students do not often perform well under competition, so is there a competitive (vs. a cooperative) learning environment? Is the teacher flexible, and does she have positive views and expectations of her students? One of the most important factors to consider is whether the curriculum matches the child's ability. If the curriculum is far too difficult for the student, he may shut down, lacking any hope of being able to perform. Oddly, though, if the curriculum is far too easy for the student, he may also shut down, this time out of sheer boredom and frustration. The curriculum therefore needs to provide the right level of challenge—not so much as to cause frustration, but enough to enable the student to learn and grow academically.

Helping the Underachieving Child

How does a caring parent or teacher set about helping a gifted student deal with underachievement issues? The first step is to determine whether the child is really underachieving—is there a gap between the student's abilities and her academic performance? While dealing with this issue, we must be willing to see the student's abilities for what they truly are, and the most dangerous mistake a parent may make here is evaluating the child incorrectly. Evaluating abilities as too advanced may lead to unrealistic expectations for the child, but evaluating abilities as too low may lead to accepting a level of challenge that is clearly too easy. For these reasons, it is best to rely on standardized assessments such as aptitude tests (e.g., intelligence tests) combined with achievement tests (e.g., SAT or CAT tests). Creativity tests and grades are also important indicators.

If parents, teachers, and counselors make the determination that the child is underachieving, the next step is to understand what is at the root of the underachievement. From there, the course of action is different depending on the cause. For example, if one student underachieves because of poor study skills, a positive course of action for him is to enroll him in a course on study skills and then for both the teacher and parent to monitor the study routine, reinforcing positive skills and discouraging negative behaviors. On the other hand, if a student underachieves because she is coping with an emotionally difficult situation at home, it would obviously benefit the student to receive counseling and support from parents and teachers to help her deal with the home situation. Sometimes, of course, more than one cause exists, complicating the matter. See the appendix of this book for additional resources that may help you to understand the causes of underachievement in gifted children and strategies for coping with it.

No matter the cause, though, parents can impart three very important ideas to their children:

> 1. *Learning can be enjoyable and useful.*
> 2. *The classroom should be (and can be) a supportive and friendly learning environment.*
> 3. *Children's developing skills and abilities will enable them to achieve.*[26]

Students who achieve generally do so because they see learning as enjoyable and/or useful—that is, they are engaged in learning because they are interested in the topic, and/or they see it as useful in their lives or as something that will help them attain their goals. Parents should communicate with their children's teachers to ensure that, at least some of the time, children are allowed to pursue their interests at school. Discussing what the child has learned over the dinner table and helping her to see how it applies to the real world will enable her to understand that learning is useful. Developing intrinsic motivation is also important. Extrinsic rewards such as prizes and stickers have their place at home or in the classroom, but only in a limited fashion. Students need experiences that teach them that learning is engaging, useful, and enjoyable for its own sake.

Similarly, all children have a right to attend a school in which the classroom is supportive and friendly, which means a place where they feel safe to make mistakes. Unfortunately, underachievers often view school as negative or even hostile, for they have come to view the classroom as a place where the teacher doesn't understand them. The first action that needs to be taken here is to determine to what extent this is true. Discussions between the parents, teachers, and the child will help. At these discussions, students should be asked to explain their concerns and helped to understand what things are in their control versus what things are outside of their power to control. Some accommodations may be made on both sides.

Finally, it is important that parents impart an awareness that their children are "up to the job" of learning. Many gifted underachieving children receive continual messages at home and at school that they are constant disappointments—failures of the system. Parents who tell their children that they believe in their abilities, even when those same children aren't performing well, are communicating the message that ability is about more than current behavior—an important message for these children to absorb. Saying to them, "This should be easy for you," is not nearly as helpful as saying, "I know that you can do this, and I'm going to be your ally to help you make it happen."

Table 2.1. Parenting Strategies to Deal with Underachievement in Gifted Children

✔ Determine whether underachievement is present. Consider the results of a variety of assessments.

✔ Diagnose causes of underachievement: student, family, or school-related.

✔ Develop a course of action that addresses the root cause(s) of the specific case.

✔ Communicate with your child's school about issues of concern. Involve the child in the discussions.

✔ Ensure that the child's classroom is an environment that is supportive and friendly.

✔ Communicate to your child that learning is enjoyable and useful.

✔ Communicate to your child your belief in his abilities.

Afterword by Josh

I'd like to start by telling the reader that although I had issues with underachievement in elementary and middle school, as my mother described, as I grew older, I figured out some of the reasons for that behavior and was able to manage it. I found that I could apply myself to things I knew I could do well and activities that interested me—but I will save that conversation for another chapter. For now, I'd like to focus on the science fair/ear-pulling incident.

While I don't remember this event quite so colorfully, I do remember that sinking feeling in my gut that appeared all too often when I was going through those middle and early high school years. It's important to understand the differences in attitudes that my sisters and I had toward school. While my sisters were plagued by anxiety that they might get a B+ in a class, my fears arose from sliding down into the cracks, somewhere in between desperately wanting to have the ambition and drive of my older sisters and "fitting in" with the rest of my peers who had not been identified as gifted.

Being a teenager is hard, plain and simple. And almost no teenager's life is worry-free, and if it is, then that might be the luckiest person to ever go through puberty. A huge problem that sat in the back of my mind was a growing fear that I wasn't actually gifted. My mom tells me that I scored well on an IQ test. To be honest, I never felt smarter than anyone else; I just knew I could spend less time learning something and get away with it.

The years that I spent in middle school doing the bare minimum of work started to catch up with me. By the time I was in high school, I could no longer do my homework right before class and get away with it. I wanted to take the time to learn the subject, but I never actually followed through with it. Procrastination was the name of the game. I would put off a project or a paper until the last moment, and it just kept sinking deeper and deeper into my consciousness. I could hear my parents lecturing me, sitting me down, and telling me the same things I had heard from them and everyone else about lying and procrastination and trustworthiness, but I kept doing the same things. I had almost zero interest in the subjects. As a 17-year-old, I couldn't imagine that there might actually be real-world applications to science and English outside of the obvious professions. (Little did I know that a few years later I would use the physics and calculus I learned in high school on a daily basis in sound design and filmmaking.) When my parents asked me why I had waited until the week after the project was due to tell them about it, I always had the same response: "I don't know." And I genuinely did not understand why I kept repeating these behaviors.

My parents handled my underachievement as best they could. They were accustomed to two highly motivated daughters who gladly finished their schoolwork on time and with a smile on their faces. There was a lot of tension between my parents and me as I became a teenager, and almost all of it stemmed from this issue. I wasn't a problem child. I never drank or smoked. I didn't sneak out of the house. To be honest, if you compared me to most other teenagers, you would find that I was a pretty good kid. And my parents recognized that, but they also knew that I could do better.

Through a series of talks and disagreements, my parents and I worked through my issues with schoolwork. We slowly came to understand what it was that motivated me to learn. I eventually found a love for music and filmmaking, which led to me going to NYU's Tisch School of the Arts. As we look back on that time now, my parents and I can laugh with each other about it.

While underachievement may seem like an insurmountable problem, it's important to understand that parents can help. Your child probably cannot even attempt to tackle it without your help. If my parents had simply walked away from the situation or had not even bothered to notice, then I would not be where I am today. I'm grateful that they intervened and pushed me and showed me that they wanted to help when it would have been just as easy for them to let me fend for myself. So at the risk of sounding like a public service announcement: Take the time to talk to your children. Every day. It will pay off in the end.

CHAPTER 3

Don't Be Silly! There's Nothing to Be Afraid Of!

Fear and Anxiety in Gifted Children

*Courage is resistance to fear, mastery of fear—not
absence of fear.*

~Mark Twain

I heard the door close behind Jen as she raced into the kitchen after
school, and with one glance at my six-year-old daughter's face, I
knew there was a problem. Instead of the glowing smile I had come
to love or the incessant chatter about her day, Jen had a furrowed
brow and tears welling up in her eyes.

"What's the matter?" I cooed, sure that the answer would be
that she had tripped and fallen or that her favorite toy was missing.
Hesitantly, she raised warm brown eyes to mine.

"Mommy," she asked in a little voice, "What's a black hole?
Can it eat us?"

I examined my daughter's furrowed brow and trembling lips,
spotting the indicators of fear. You could have knocked me over
with a feather. Black holes? What does a six-year-old know about
black holes? And why would she be afraid of them?

Two possible responses came to mind: (1) I could say, "Don't be silly! Why are you afraid?" or (2) I could acknowledge what seemed to be genuine fear and help my child understand and deal with it. As a parent, I have not always made the best choices, but on this occasion I'm happy to report that I knew enough to discard the first option and choose instead option #2.

"Sweetie," I replied, "where did you hear about black holes, and what makes you think they will eat us?"

Jen's gaze was serious and steady as she replied, "We learned about them in class today, and a boy said that they're so strong they pull everything around them in. Are there any black holes near us? Can they eat us?"

Sighing, I thought about how to respond.

How many times have we as adults been confronted by a fear? Telling ourselves that fear is silly often doesn't work. I have experienced times when I was driving home alone in the dark and imagined that there was a prowler lurking in the backseat. In these instances, I reasoned with myself that the fear was silly. Hadn't I seen the empty backseat when I entered the car? Children, however, are different. As a parent talking to my six-year-old, I had not yet discovered the social-emotional research behind dealing with children's fears and anxieties. But I did have the instinct and personal experience—especially experience—to know that making light of my child's fear was not the right approach.

Frequently, gifted children are highly imaginative. Children with this type of vivid imagination may battle fears, but oftentimes, the fears are imagined. For example, I was the child who couldn't sleep because an imaginary monster was in my closet. My mother would hear me cry out, enter my room, turn on the light, look in the closet, and then assure me that the monster was not real. As soon as she left, though, the monster would return to the closet and keep me awake all night. I also feared disease, and whenever I watched a medically-oriented television show, I'd be convinced that I had whatever disease was featured. My parents, as loving as they were, didn't know how to handle these fears, and they asked me why I was so afraid. This approach never worked because I could not tell them *why*, and so I took to hiding more and more of my fears. Of course, that didn't help anything either. It was only after I became an adult that I developed some coping mechanisms for dealing with fear.

I knew as I listened to my daughter talk about her fear that I couldn't call it silly. To do so would have been to invalidate the fear, and it would not help her learn how to cope with it. So carefully, thoughtfully, I said to Jen, "Tell me everything you know about black holes."

Jen narrated a long string of facts and pseudo-facts, some learned in class, some learned through reading, and some picked up in her discussions with other children. Evidently, black holes were a hot topic at school. After I understood what she did and did not know, I set about correcting some of her misinformation.

"First of all," I replied," there aren't that many powerful black holes in our galaxy. At least, scientists don't think there are. There may be miniature black holes, but they are too small to swallow up anything. The big ones are far away from the Earth." My daughter searched my face to make sure I was telling the truth. Satisfied, she turned away from me, running off toward the kitchen. "Are there any cookies?" she asked.

Overexcitabilities

In 1964, a researcher named Kazimierz Dabrowski[27] theorized that some individuals possess *overexcitabilities*, or a heightened sensitivity to their surroundings. Dabrowski thought that this extreme sensitivity was actually caused by an increased neuronal response to stimuli. It is important to realize that Dabrowski did not consider this super-sensitivity to be a disorder, but rather a positive trait that eventually leads to advanced development in the individual. Dabrowski theorized that gifted children possess more of these overexcitabilities than most children.

What is life like for a gifted child with overexcitabilities? Probably the best adjective to describe it is "heightened," for the individual has a heightened intensity, awareness, and sensitivity to life experiences. She might cry while reading a poem because she can feel the emotion that is generated by the words. She might be more afraid than most others of a particularly scary ghost story. Or a black hole.

Dabrowski went on to outline five areas in which overexcitability might occur: psychomotor, sensual, intellectual, emotional, and imaginational. Children who demonstrate psychomotor overexcitability simply love to move; they have a surplus of energy, are often physically active, speak rapidly, need to act, and can't sit still. Sensually overexcitable children experience a heightened sense of pleasure or displeasure from their senses—sight, smell, touch, taste, and hearing, such as children who get unusually great delight from tastes or smells, or children who can't stand to have tags in their shirts or get their hands dirty because of the sensation it causes. Intellectually overexcitable children seek answers and demand truth and justice, and they are often the children who are always asking questions and challenging adults to provide evidence for the answers. For emotionally overexcitable children, life can be difficult, because they are acutely aware of and sensitive to their own and others' emotions. Their compassion, empathy, and sensitivity may lead them to form intense relationships or, on the other hand, to be cautious and shy with others. Children with imaginational overexcitability may daydream and love to create imaginary worlds. Sometimes they may even have trouble distinguishing between fact and fiction and often are quite dramatic even about simple tasks. They may be bored in a class that doesn't hold their interest and may draw or write stories to fill the time. It is almost as if they live in their heads—in a dream world of their own.

It is not difficult to see how overexcitabilities can lead to anxieties and fears in gifted children. For example, a child with imaginational overexcitability may read a newspaper or Internet article about an outbreak of the virulent Ebola virus in a country far away and instantly imagine it spreading to his hometown, with devastating consequences. The emotionally excitable child may interpret an off-hand comment that someone in his class made about him and dwell on it for weeks, turning it over and over in his mind, worrying about its meaning. Sensually overexcitable children may experience anxiety in a crowded, noisy room. It becomes apparent why some gifted children are described as "too sensitive," "too intense," "too emotional," or "too anxious." Yet this is a part of their makeup. Their overexcitabilities on the one hand can be a hindrance, but on the other hand, they provide the passion, excitement, and drive to master activities that far exceed those found in other children.

Asynchronous Development

A second phenomenon that comes into play with gifted children that may lead to anxiety or fear is the concept of *asynchronous development.*[28] "Asynchronous" literally means "out of synch," conveying the idea that some gifted children's abilities may develop faster or slower than others. These include intellectual abilities, emotional abilities, and physical abilities, all of which can develop at different rates. This uneven development may lead to emotional difficulties in gifted children in several ways. For example, a child with advanced intellectual abilities but age-normal emotional abilities might be able to read material that is intended for a much older audience. She may intellectually comprehend the storyline of a frightening suspense novel, but this does not mean that she is emotionally ready to be exposed to the more graphic parts of the story, which may conjure up scary images in her young mind. Or a child with advanced intellectual abilities (and imaginational overexcitabilities) might concoct an entire story in his head from start to finish, but because his physical development may lag, he can't put pen to paper (or fingers to keyboard) fast enough to get the story out, causing him to cry in frustration.

Asynchronous development, then, may be another cause for some gifted children's fears and anxieties. Additionally, parents should be aware that asynchronous development often increases with IQ and may be more prevalent in twice-exceptional students, or students who are both gifted and possess some other exceptionality such as a learning disability.[29]

Teaching Your Child How to Deal with Fears and Anxieties

It is important for adults to remember that although over-excitabilities and asynchrony can contribute to fear and anxiety in gifted children, they offer blessings as well. Heightened awareness and sensitivity to the world around them and our fellow human beings afford gifted children the opportunity to live life to the fullest and make a positive impact through purposeful lives. The question is not how to eliminate heightened awareness and sensitivities, but rather how to enable gifted children to rise above their fears for the purpose of freeing them to enjoy their life to the fullest and realize their full potential.

Every child experiences some fears or anxieties, and I have compiled a set of five steps or strategies for dealing with them. Because gifted children's fears can be more extreme than those of average-ability children, it is important to consider their frequency and severity. How often does your child experience her fears, and how debilitating are they in the course of her life? If the fears interfere with daily activities, if they frequently disturb the child's sleep at night, or if you notice undue emotional distress even after attempting the five steps I describe in this section, it is time to seek professional help. Several excellent professional models have been developed for dealing with the social-emotional difficulties of gifted children. Some of these are listed in the appendix, along with other resources to help you deal with your child's fears.

If you do choose counseling, it will be important to select the right counselor. It is unfortunate that many counselors are unfamiliar with the needs of gifted children or the special social-emotional issues that may present themselves among the gifted. You'll want to ask your family members, friends, and other parents of gifted children for recommendations. When you find a counselor, attend the first session with your child, and observe the counselor-child dynamic. Don't be afraid to ask about the counselor about his or her knowledge of giftedness and relevant issues, such as perfectionism or underachievement.[30] Perhaps the most important questions to ask are: "Do you believe that there are gifted children?" "Could giftedness be a component in what is going on with my child?" "What do you think it's like to be a gifted child?" "Do gifted children deal with any special emotional issues?" The answers will tell you reams.

If the fears and anxieties are not debilitating, you might try the following steps.

Step 1. Listen and observe

Perhaps the most important thing you can do to help your gifted child deal with fear and anxiety is to accept and understand his feelings. Observe his actions, and listen as he tells you his concerns. Really listen, focus, and concentrate on him alone. Observe his body posture. Is he tense? Watch his facial expressions. All of these are signs of the degree of the anxiety. When my children were anxious, it's as if they were tightly wound little springs, ready to release at any minute. Ask questions, but do it gently. Let him be the guide through his fears. Don't ask, "But *why* do you feel that way?" Say instead, "I want you to help me understand what you are afraid of so that I can help. Tell me all about what you're afraid of and why you're afraid of it."

Sometimes children don't want to open up and talk about their fears. If so, be patient and don't insist. Try letting a little time go by; then involve the child in an activity that you can do together. For example, you might try having the child help you with a routine household chore. While you're washing veggies in the kitchen, for example, you might talk and casually bring up the fear issue. "I noticed earlier that you seemed upset about something. Want to talk about it?" Sometimes taking the focus off of the conversation and onto a shared activity helps children open up.

Step 2. Acknowledge the fear or anxiety, and establish yourself as an ally

Once you have an understanding of the fear or anxiety, it's time to reassure your child that it's okay. Many anxious gifted children think that they should be braver, sensing that they are more fearful than other children—a thought process which may lead to more anxiety. Not only must they deal with the fear, but now they must deal with the shame of feeling that way.

If the fear is a realistic one (e.g., war), you might try saying, "You know, many people, even adults, are afraid of this, and so it's natural for you to be afraid of this, too." If the fear is a less realistic one (e.g., a monster under the bed), you could take a different approach, saying instead, "People are afraid of many different things. I have things that I'm afraid of, so it doesn't surprise me that you're afraid sometimes, too. That's okay."

End this step by establishing yourself as an ally with your child—someone she can turn to when she is beset by fears or anxieties. Let her know that you'll always be there, and she can always talk with you. Say, for example, "I want to help you with this, and I want you to know that you can always talk to me about this or anything else."

Step 3. Help the child understand the nature of the problem, and emphasize the positive

Once you've listened, acknowledged the fear or anxiety, and set yourself up as an ally, you will want to begin helping your child reason through the concern. The strategy here depends on the age of the child. For very young children, it's probably enough to help them distinguish between reality and fantasy. If the problem is a monster in the room, the room should be searched thoroughly. If the problem is more realistic, such as a black hole, even very young children can understand reasons why something is not likely to happen. In my conversation with my daughter, I emphasized the fact that large black holes are very far away and not likely to come close to Earth, and smaller black holes are not powerful enough to do any harm. The likelihood of such an event occurring is also a good thing to discuss. Tell your child that the thing he fears is about as likely to happen as finding one particular grain of sand buried on the beach among all of the others.

Older children will probably be able to reason in a much more sophisticated manner, but the strategy is still the same. Discuss the details of the fear, emphasizing the positive. Focus on the facts that make the fear less frightening, such as the small probability of something dire happening. Never lie to a child, though. Be honest if the situation calls for it, but always bring the line of reasoning back to where you can emphasize the positive. You might even agree to research the concern together, using the Internet or the library to find more information. By doing this, you're not only helping your child to deal with the fear, but you're also demonstrating that her concern is important to you.

Step 4. Reassure and decompress

After you've helped your child reason through his fear, you need to reassure him that you're there for him—now and in the future—and that you will protect him. Children crave stability in their lives, and as a parent, it is our role to be the stable adult who helps them through their fears and anxieties. Encourage your child to come to you should his fear persist. Also, watch for signs that the fear is diminishing, which might include a relaxing of the muscles in the child's body, a softening of facial expressions, and a slowing of breathing. These are all indicators that the child is decompressing.

You might also try teaching your child some relaxation techniques. One easy (and very effective) method is to practice breathing slowly, deeply, and consciously, counting 1-2-3-4-5 with the intake breath, holding it for a bit, and then matching the same count for the outtake breath, continuing this process for five minutes or more until the child's rapid breathing is gone. Another relaxation exercise is to lie on the bed or the floor and tense all of the muscles, hold for 5-10 seconds, then let go, and repeat this several times, ending with all muscles totally relaxed. After five minutes of alternate tension and relaxation, your child's body should be less tense. Teaching strategies like these can help children learn to calm their fears. If your child responds to physical touch, a good shoulder massage, backrub, or head-massage can also do wonders.

Step 5. Divert the child

Once you see that the fear has drained away from your child, it can be helpful to use some type of diversion to refocus her attention onto something more positive. An appropriate diversion will vary for each child. Some children respond to humor, some to games played with an adult, and some to physical cuddling. Whatever your child responds to, it's important to find the thing that will take her mind off of the fear. Finding something that you can do together is best, as it will reinforce your presence, love, and support.

A wonderful example of taking a child's mind away from fear is depicted in a scene from the movie *Little Man Tate*. In the movie, Jody Foster plays the mother of a young, highly gifted child named Fred, who often awakens with nightmares. In the scene, Fred has just had a nightmare about a disease that prematurely ages people. He is convinced that he has the disease. His mother helps Fred deal with the fear, and then she crawls into bed with him and plays a game with him in which they watch shadows on the ceiling and name what the shadows look like. Reassured, Fred is able to fall back to sleep.

Table 3.1. Parenting Strategies to Deal with Fears and Anxieties in Gifted Children

✔ Determine if your child's fears and anxieties are too frequent and/or debilitating. If they are, seek professional counseling.

✔ When dealing with your child's fear or anxiety, listen and observe carefully.

✔ Acknowledge the fear or anxiety, and set yourself up as an ally to your child.

✔ Help your child understand the fear or anxiety, emphasizing the positive.

✔ Reassure your child, and help her to decompress.

✔ Divert your child's attention to something else.

Afterword by Jen

I don't remember this story at all, but it does sound like me. Apparently, Mom did such a great job of reassuring me that I got over my childhood fear of black holes. My adult fear, however, is another story. When my college astronomy professor mentioned in passing that a miniature version of a black hole was theoretically possible, it bothered me. I called my boyfriend, a budding astrophysicist, to joke about my fear, but also frankly to seek some reassurance. He responded with admirable restraint to what was not a normal thing for a grown woman to fear. His consistently calm reaction to my least rational worries is something that he has in common with my parents, and it's one of the reasons I love him (and married him).

I make light of my fears, but the truth is that it's something I've struggled to manage my whole life. When I was younger, I worried about everything from black holes to whether I would finish my homework. Then I worried about why I was so fearful.

Now I worry about more common things, such as whether I left the oven on or the keys in the car, and I don't beat myself up as often about being fearful or anxious. I've accepted that it's just the way I am, even though I often wish I could be different. One of the major themes of this book is acceptance—your acceptance of your child's basic character and needs, and your ability to encourage her to accept herself. It is certainly painful to live with a tendency toward anxiety, and it's only natural to want to spare your child that pain.

For me, though, it was only *more* painful to add to my anxieties the strain of trying to be different than I was. Accepting that I am a worrier has allowed me to seek out a support network and strategies for managing my stress. And there's more. Properly approached, my fears have paradoxically made me freer than I might otherwise have been. It sounds strange, but I've come (in my most optimistic moments) to view my anxiety as a gift.

You see, as I said, I usually worry about run-of-the-mill things, but every so often, I end up in a situation that makes my anxiety go off the charts. A few years ago, I was in Russia on a summer research trip when a minor issue with my visa developed. I panicked, convinced that I would be stuck in a foreign country forever. Ignoring the calmer voices telling me that it wouldn't make any sense for immigration to keep me in Russia and that I was much more likely to be summarily ejected from the country, I focused on the tales of woe I had read on the Internet. Jane What's-Her-Name and her entire family had been trapped in Russia because of a problem *just like mine.* How on earth could I trust my advisor, the guidebook, and the American consulate after what I had read about Jane and her family *on the Internet?*

In the end, I went to the airport with hundreds of dollars in various currencies to pay whatever fine the passport agent might impose. She barely gave me a second glance before stamping my passport and waving me through. I was so relieved that I spent all my remaining rubles on overpriced CDs that I giddily enjoyed all the way home.

I tell this story not only because it is the most outlandish and entertaining example of my adult anxieties, but because it occurred at a pivotal point in my life. I was 21, and this was my first real solo travel experience. I had travelled by myself to visit friends and relatives, and trips alone to and from school were nothing unusual. This was different, though; this was far away, another country; no one was waiting for me at the end of the day. My first night in St. Petersburg was also the first night I had ever spent alone in a hotel. I rented an apartment, where I stayed by myself, and checked it every night for prowlers. My closest family members were in Paris, my nearest confidantes eight time zones away. Calling home was expensive and difficult, and I felt very, very alone.

My mother would tell you I went a little crazy then, and maybe she's right. I was certainly irrational, and I took some ribbing for it when I got home. It got me thinking, though: Why, without my support system, was I so vulnerable there to the overblown fears that had gripped me? And what could I do to make sure it didn't happen again?

I wasn't starting from scratch. My parents had, throughout my childhood, helped me to construct the foundations of a system that I'm still refining. Once I had a chance to process it, the visa incident showed me how to make that system work on its own, without constant support from family and friends. Sometimes I still feel the approach of a fear that threatens my ability to think rationally. It's never gotten the same hold on me again, though, even when I've had to fight it alone.

Mom and Dad taught me two things. From my mother, who has struggled with the same issues, I learned to reason through my fears. I learned to ask questions, to judge the reliability of my various sources of information, to find better ones, and to draw reasonable conclusions from them. An online forum telling Jane's story, compelling as it was, simply wasn't as reliable as the American consulate, and over time, I came to appreciate the distinction. I learned to take context and probability into account; the scientific papers that discuss miniature black holes are reputable but operate in a system outside of everyday life. Their claims that these terrors are possible don't mean that they are probable or that they are likely ever to affect me.

From my father, with his training in business and economics, I learned about fully costing my decisions. He's the one who expanded my basic high school economics example of opportunity cost ("If you go to the party, you can't go to the concert.") to include the things it usually takes many years to see. Just as I've learned to evaluate risk rationally I've come to acknowledge that fear, for all its benefits in keeping me safe and productive, also costs me something. My anxieties over the years have made me study hard, ask questions, and call home often—all good things. They've also caused me sleepless nights and the physical discomforts that come with stress. Those are the obvious costs. But how much more could I have enjoyed and done in Russia if I hadn't been fixated on solving my visa problem?

When I say that my anxieties paradoxically freed me, I'm referring to this chance I have—that your children will have, if they're lifelong worriers like I am—to face all of my fears rationally. It doesn't mean that I always make the best decisions, but I do have to judge each one on its own merits. There are a lot of "common knowledge" fears whose factual foundations are sketchy at best, but like most fears, they impose significant limitations on our lives. A worrier doesn't have the option of accepting only those common anxieties and adjusting his life accordingly. To me, there is no experiential difference between the fear of being eaten by a black hole and the fear of being attacked by a stranger at night. I have no sound way of differentiating between them.

The choice I face is to evaluate all of my fears, common and unusual, and discover whether they're reasonable or succumb to them. If I were to succumb, though, their sheer number would overwhelm me and drive out of my life anything that gives it meaning. I would be stuck in my home, alone, afraid of everything from failed relationships to meteors and anything you've ever heard as an urban legend. I would live, perhaps, a safer life, but it would be a less joyful one. My anxieties have taught me that fear is good—again, it keeps us safe—but it doesn't have to have the final say in my life. As stressful as that lesson was to learn, I'm grateful for it.

CHAPTER 4

Do It Because I Said So!

Dealing with Gifted Children's Challenges to Authority

I cannot teach anybody anything.
I can only make them think.

~Socrates

Jen had a tiny precious clock—a gift from my mother—which she kept on her nightstand. The clock was round and trimmed in gold, and it gave off a pleasant-sounding tinkling alarm. Both of my girls were fascinated with it. Jen, the older of the two, was intrigued with how to wind and set the clock. Sarah, at two, was more enthralled with the sound it made when she picked it up and threw it to the floor, a habit she practiced frequently with many objects.

Sarah's throwing obsession was a short and intense stage, but a difficult one because she grabbed whatever object caught her attention, threw it to the floor, and said in a loud voice, "Boom!" Down went her stuffed rabbit, and we'd hear, "Boom!" The rabbit hit the floor so often that we took to calling it "Boom." Next she would grab a plastic toy and throw it to the floor. "Boom!" Then came household items such as plastic dishes. "Boom!" Eventually, she focused her efforts on some of Jen's things.

When Sarah started throwing Jen's items to the floor, I wondered if it might be due to misplaced sibling hostility. But because Sarah only threw plush or plastic toys, ones that couldn't break or be hurt, I didn't take action—that is, until the night she threw the clock to the floor.

"No, no," I told Sarah. "You can't throw your sister's clock to the floor." "Why?" asked Sarah. "Because I said so," I replied. Sarah acquiesced, although I could tell she was not pleased. Later, after the girls had both had their baths and were drying off, Sarah ran into the bedroom, grabbed the clock off the nightstand, and again hurled it to the floor. "Boom!" she shouted, delighted. Like any good two-year-old, she was testing me and the limit I had set.

What happened next is an example of how even a patient parent can be pushed to the edge. My husband, who had been helping with the girls' nightly bedtime routine, broke off combing Jen's hair and picked Sarah up, taking her into the bathroom. Exasperated, he looked around, and his eye lit upon a plastic Barbie bubble-bath figure that Sarah loved. "Let me show you how it feels to have your toys thrown down to the ground," he said, grabbing the Barbie figure. "Boom!" he cried as he threw it to the floor. Stunned, Sarah looked up at him. She was quiet for a minute. Then she turned and walked away and never willfully threw a toy to the ground again.

I share this story not to suggest that this was necessarily the best way to deal with the situation. Rather, I want to illustrate that gifted children often require more than "Because I said so" as a reason either to do or not to do something. Children will test your limits, and when they do, it's important for a parent's response to be firm, reasonable, and consistent about enforcing those limits.

Challenges to Authority

It is not uncommon for gifted children to be described as argumentative or willful. These children are like sponges, picking up information from the news, from books, and from movies. They know a lot, and they may not be afraid to say so. They may also be unwilling to accept rules and facts simply because an adult says so. Unfortunately, the result is that they can get into trouble by challenging authority. It may be a teacher at school, or it may be a parent, babysitter, or other authority figure. Although these children are the ones who are often the most challenging in school and at home, they are also sometimes the ones who, if we are honest, help us to become better people because they challenge us to defend our positions. They also often possess spirit and care passionately about social issues such as fairness and justice.

In our family, Sarah was this child. I noticed her strong will, spirit, and stubbornness as early as her toddler years. As she grew older, we found more effective ways of communicating, and her father and I learned that there were times when we had to be strict and draw a line in the sand and times when we could be more permissive. We also learned that it was always better to explain our reasons than to say, "Because I said so."

Once when Sarah was about 16 and driving, she called and asked to stay out late to attend a party, which, unfortunately, was to take place at a stranger's house and would not be over until midnight. We said no. Angrily, she left the house for a movie instead. When I called to make sure she had not gone to the party, she angrily shouted into the phone, "I can see you don't trust me!"

As she made her way home, her father and I discussed how we would handle the situation when Sarah walked in the door. We agreed that we trusted her with many responsibilities, but we had to get this point across without backtracking on our position on the party at a stranger's home. When she came through the door, we were ready.

"I can't believe you called to check up on me," she fumed.

"We do trust you about things that you're ready to handle."

"Oh yeah? Really?" she challenged.

"Really," replied her father. "But if you don't feel that we trust you, maybe we should take away the things that we do trust you about."

"What do you mean?" Sarah looked at us guardedly.

"Well," said Fred, "you can start by returning the car keys. The fact that we provide a car for you to drive says we trust you to be responsible. Also, please hand back the debit card that we gave you to use in emergencies. We definitely don't give our debit card to people that we don't trust. Oh, and there's your cell phone...."

For once, my usually composed daughter looked totally nonplussed. Sensing that we had the advantage of the argument, she retreated to her room, giving us a gloomy backward look as she closed her bedroom door. The next morning, the storm was over, and I sensed that we had made a little progress on the trust issue.

Our other children exhibited some of the same passion about various issues—especially if they felt they were right. This passion can be valuable in the right context. In an adult, passion may translate into a spirit for life, but in children, it can be frustrating, especially for the teacher whose authority or knowledge is challenged or the parent who has to learn how to communicate with the gifted child. It can be difficult to learn to avoid saying those four tempting words, "Because I said so."

Reasons Why Gifted Students Challenge Authority

What are the reasons behind some gifted children's opposition to authority, and what are some strategies for dealing with it? You may recall from Chapter 3 that many gifted children have fears that result from asynchrony and overexcitabilities. These two factors also come into play in children who challenge authority. Consider the child who is intellectually advanced (and intellectually overexcitable) but who is emotionally at a level appropriate for his age. This child stays up late at night reading about, for example, global warming; he has a passion for the topic and knows far more than his teacher does on the subject. In fact, the teacher may not know many of the individual topics that she teaches in such depth. During a class discussion on global warming, this student may correct her on a particular fact, and he may do so in such a way that he misses the look of annoyance on her face. Worse, he may do this repeatedly throughout the lesson. Often, it's not the fact that a student has corrected her to which the teacher objects—it is the way in which it's done.

This teacher must now decide between two courses of action: she may defy the student, sticking to her information in order to save face, or she may acknowledge that the student is (or might be) correct. An experienced teacher who understands gifted students almost always chooses the latter course, but she will probably talk with the student after class about when and how it is appropriate to interrupt. In a worse-case scenario, if the teacher is inexperienced with or lacks knowledge of reasons for gifted students' "defiance," she may choose to oppose the student, which can end in a nasty power struggle and bitter feelings. I have heard of extreme cases in which these kinds of teachers set about publicly humiliating the student in front of the class in an effort to regain control. When you consider that some gifted students are also emotionally intense or sensitive, it is not difficult to understand how this type of experience can make bright, sensitive children cringe, resent their teachers, and even hate school.

Gifted children's defiance can also stem from their heightened awareness of social justice.[31] In elementary school, children begin to develop a sense of what is right and wrong, fair and unfair, and some gifted children are keenly aware of these issues. They may worry about the poor and ask their parents if they can give money to homeless people on the street. They engage in debates at school and with activities that focus on social action. They also sometimes can't (or won't) accept school or home rules if teachers or parents say, "Because I told you so." They must be given reasons why a rule exists, and then they are much more likely to accept—and maybe even "buy into"—the rule.

I learned this the hard way when I first started teaching gifted elementary students. I taught 25 eager, gifted fourth graders in a small portable classroom tucked away on a back lot of the local elementary school. Each and every day, my students poured through the doors of that portable, eager and ready to learn. At the time, though, I had much to learn about teaching gifted students, and this became readily apparent during the first days of class when I noticed that many of my students were very aware of issues regarding what was fair and what was not fair.

Any educator needs a way to manage behavior in the classroom, and being a fairly new teacher, I decided that the best way to reward good behavior and discourage poor behavior was through a ticket system. I purchased a roll of tickets—the type you get at a movie theater—and told the students that they could earn tickets through good behavior. Cleaning up after activities and working for extended periods of time, for example, earned students a ticket. Tickets could then be turned in at a later time for treats such as small toys or candy. Students vigorously embraced this extrinsic reward system, at least for a few days. After a while, though, several students noticed that I did not (and indeed, could not) be totally consistent in how I awarded the tickets. If I was in a good mood, tickets might be given more liberally, but if it had been a tough day, I might become stingy with my distribution of the coveted tickets. Several students complained, "That's not fair!" I tried to equalize my distribution of the tickets, but the system soon broke down completely as I realized that I could never accomplish complete fairness with the tickets in the classroom.

The uneven distribution of tickets wasn't the students' only concern about fairness. Any classroom issue became a potential hotbed of contention that raised students' hackles. If I asked students to do homework over the weekend after telling them I didn't usually assign weekend homework, I would hear, "That's not fair!" If I gave back two papers and they received different grades for what the students felt was the same amount of work, the cry went out, "That's not fair!" Soon, almost any issue raised the clarion call, until nearly all students were taking advantage of the situation. I finally resorted to (you guessed it) banning the words "That's not fair!" I actually took to penalizing students who uttered the prohibited words. Later, as tensions eased, it became a classroom joke, and all I had to do was look at students a certain way if they started to say the words and the whole class would burst into laughter. As I gained teaching experience, I learned more effective ways of dealing with these gifted children's defiance of authority and their concern for social justice.

Solving the Problem

So what have I learned over the years as a parent and a teacher that I might pass along about dealing with the issue of defiance of authority? First, I learned that it's important to gain buy-in from the child, and buy-in means either that the child believes that the decision or rule is a good one because it make sense or because she herself has thought of it. For small children, it's simple. I remember when Jen went through the terrible twos. Like so many two-year-olds, the word she seized upon and wouldn't let go of was "No!" Everything was "No!" Every question, every demand, every sentence out of my mouth was met with "No!" It was actually funny sometimes, especially when I would say, "Do you want to…," and before I could get out the rest of the sentence, I would hear a resounding "No!" from my daughter. I would then finish the sentence, "…go get ice cream?" Puzzled, she would stare at me, certain that she'd made a mistake, but unsure of how or why it had happened. Later, I learned that it helped if I gave her a choice. Instead of starting sentences with the words, "Would you like to…," I began, "Would you rather…." "Would you rather wear the blue pants or the red pants?" "Would you rather eat peas or carrots for dinner?" The idea here was that with limited choices (that I had already approved in my mind), my young daughter could select one, thereby feeling that she had some control over the situation.

With older children, gaining buy-in is a little more difficult. Certainly, the approach described above still works, but frequently, children who are elementary age and older will balk unless you also explain your thinking. Instead, you'll have to gain buy-in another way, and it's generally good to make the rule or come to the decision together. Use the Problem-Solver Contract in Figure 4.1 to work through these steps. As you're completing the steps, fill out the form together. Taking the time to write your ideas down sometimes defuses the situation.

Figure 4.1. Problem-Solver Contract*

Problem or concern from parent's point of view:	Problem or concern from child's point of view:
Parent's objective(s):	Child's objective(s):

Final solution:
Parent will do:
Child will do:

Consequences for breaking the contract
Parent:
Child:

Consequences for keeping the contract:

Agreed	Agreed
Parent's Signature:	Child's Signature:
Date:	Date:

* This contract is adapted from Osborne's six-step problem-solving process and typical contracts found in teacher books.

The form can be completed by one parent and one child, or two parents, or even the whole family can be involved. Eventually, all of your children will likely have their chance to have one of their problems solved using this six-step process.

Step 1. Describe the problem

First, sit with your child and describe the problem or concern from your point of view. Then, listen to your child as he describes the problem from his point of view. Encourage eye contact, and listen—really listen.

Step 2. Focus on objectives

Focus on the objectives that each of you wants. For example, if the problem is that your teenage daughter doesn't get enough cell phone time and she's upset, the underlying objective for you might be to save the cost of the cell phone minutes, or it might be to have her grades improve as she spends less time on the phone and more time hitting the books. The underlying objective for her is probably to stay in touch with her friends. This process of focusing on the underlying objective is helpful because it clarifies what the true concern is. In this example, the parent's concern might be cost or it might be grades—two very different concerns which need to be addressed differently.

There may be times when your child's objectives are unrealistic or unsafe. For example, if your son wants to stay out until midnight on a school night, you may reasonably argue that the time is too late. Try to get at the real underlying objective. Perhaps it's that he feels that you don't trust him, and he wants that trust. Are there other ways in which that objective may be met? Keep working at it together until you understand the real issues and how they may be shaped into one or more objectives that are palatable to both you and your child.

Step 3. Brainstorm possibilities for solutions

Brainstorming is a technique developed by marketing guru Alex Osborne[32] that is used successfully today in the corporate world, the classroom, and many other settings to generate ideas and possible solutions to problems. You and your child can use it, too, to generate solutions that meet both your and her objectives. It's important to understand the rules of brainstorming: don't criticize or judge ideas, and write down as many ideas as possible that you can in the time allotted (say, three minutes). It's helpful to ask someone who is not involved with the process to be the timekeeper. Then, simply think of (and write down) as many ideas as possible.

For example, let's say that your daughter likes to play music in her room in the evenings, but the music seems to be getting louder, and she seems to be playing it later and later. Her younger brother is beginning to complain about being distracted while trying to complete his homework. Some ideas for solving this problem might include:

- ✔ No music after 9:00 p.m.

- ✔ Music may be played only at a certain digital volume setting.

- ✔ Music may be played at a certain digital volume setting before 9:00 p.m. or on the weekends, but then afterward, it must decrease to a lower volume setting.

- ✔ Parents will buy earplugs.

Okay, that last one was a bit tongue-in-cheek, but you get the idea. Participants may either brainstorm separately, writing their ideas in silence on the brainstorming form in Figure 4.2 and then comparing lists, or together, calling out ideas and recording them on the form. Again, remember that the point of brainstorming is not to judge ideas, merely to write them down. Evaluation comes in the next step.

Figure 4.2. Brainstorming

Parent's Ideas	Advantages	Disadvantages
•		
•		
•		
•		
•		
•		
•		
Child's Ideas	Advantages	Disadvantages
•		
•		
•		
•		
•		
•		
•		

Step 4. Evaluate ideas and select a final solution

For each idea, think of and list (on the same form) all of the advantages and disadvantages that the idea offers your child and your family. Let's look at another example. Suppose you have recorded an idea that your teenager cannot spend all of his allowance at the movies but instead must put 20% of it into savings. Two advantages might be that he will save money, perhaps for college or for a special purchase such as a desired electronic device, and he may learn more about financial responsibility. A disadvantage might be that he might have to wait to go to the movies with his friends.

Remember that it's important to write the advantages and disadvantages to both the child and other family members. Returning to the example of the loud music, if the music interferes with Dad's sleep because he works a night shift and sleeps during the day, then the child's solution of playing her music loudly only during the day is a definite disadvantage (and possibly a deal-breaker) for Dad.

Once you have gone through this process for both your and your child's ideas, you will need some time to review and discuss the possibilities. Some solutions may be more palatable than others. When you and your child agree, it is easy to pick a final solution. More likely, there will be some amount of compromise on both parts before you reach that solution.

If your child is not cooperative, it may be necessary to narrow the solutions down to two or three that are acceptable to you. Make sure at least one idea, even if modified, comes from your child's list. Then say the following: "I'm the adult, and I am responsible for what goes on in this house. I also want what's best for you. We've spent quite a bit of time developing these ideas, so I welcome your input and encourage you to help me pick one of these solutions. If you decide not to participate, I will be sad, but I will have to continue and select one of the solutions on my own. So will you help me, or shall I just pick the solution that makes the most sense to me?" By doing this, you empower your child, and yet you begin to constrain the outcome. Once a solution is selected, record it on the Problem-Solver Contract form.

It is important that the solution be specific, outlining the actions that both the parents and the child will take. For example, suppose the problem is that the child is staying up too late and is tired in school, resulting in poor grades. However, the child believes that he is capable of staying up an hour later, and so the solution might be to institute a compromise consisting of a test period in which the child stays up 30 minutes later. The specific action for the child might be to turn off the lights and be in bed at 9:30 p.m. (as opposed to 9:00 p.m.), while the specific action for the parents might be to regularly monitor homework and grades to make sure the child is retaining at least a B average. Record the specific actions that each party will take in the Problem-Solver Contract.

Step 5. Agree to consequences and rewards

In real life, contracts are not contracts without consequences and rewards. These must be reasonable, do-able, and agreed to by all involved parties. If you agree to pay a monthly mortgage on your house and don't follow through, the house may be repossessed. If you do make the monthly payments on time, you keep the house and eventually own the house free and clear. Consequences and rewards help guide and shape our behaviors so that we follow the contract. Therefore, it is advisable to develop reasonable and do-able consequences with which both you and your child can live.

What does it mean for consequences and rewards to be "reasonable" and "do-able?" It means that they should be within your reach to provide. I can't tell you how many times I've heard angry parents shout at their children when they are misbehaving in the grocery store, "If you don't stop, I'm going to lock you by yourself in the car!" I cringe when I hear this because it is almost certain that the parent will *not* do this due to the fact that this places the child in danger. In some states, it is illegal. If you threaten something you can't or won't do, it sends a message to the child that your words mean nothing. If, on the other hand, you promise a consequence or reward that you can deliver and you follow through on it, then your child comes to understand that you mean what you say, and what you promise will probably happen. This trust is important for your child to learn if she is to develop good relationships in her own life. It's a part of respect. It means that if you make a promise, whether something positive or negative, you will follow through.

For example, suppose the problem is that your 10-year-old child spends his allowance too quickly, comes to you for more, and is angry if you won't give it to him. You work through the process described here and decide together that the solution is that you will provide him with extra chores around the house to earn more money. Let's imagine that you also decide that part of the solution will be that he can't ask for money between allowances, and if he does, you will never give him another penny. Is this consequence reasonable? No! You know that you are going to have to give him more funds—after all, he may be living with you for several more years! This is a consequence that is doomed from the start, and both of you know it. A more reasonable and logical consequence might be that if he asks for money again before the next allowance, you will pay him slightly less for the chores that he does. A reward might be that if he goes a week without asking for more money, you will pay him slightly more.

Step 6. Sign the contract

The last step in the contract process is to sign the contract, an action that indicates that both parties are in agreement with the details of the contract. Don't skip this step. It makes the process carry more weight, and later on down the road, it makes it more enforceable. It also makes it difficult for either party to claim that he or she didn't understand something in the contract. Make sure your child understands the contract. Read it out loud, or have your child read it. Be sure to review the fine points of the solution, as well as the consequences. Ask your child if she is ready to sign. Then sign and date the contract—in ink. A contract is a good way to teach children some accountability. If they do this, such and such will result. If not, there will be another result. This is the way the world works. There are consequences for our actions.

Getting along with your child and establishing good lines of communication is about much more than developing a contract.

The contract is for when times get tough and there are difficulties already. However, the old saying about prevention being better than a cure is especially applicable here. You can make much more headway with your child during times of crisis if you have built a solid everyday foundation, and the best way to do this is to spend time with your child when neither of you is upset. It doesn't have to be every day, but it has to occur sometimes. It's good if you can do something that both of you like, such as biking, hiking, shopping, or going to a movie.

My husband and I used to try to get one of the children alone periodically with one or both of us for just such an activity. We called it "special time," and we went out and had fun with just one child—no siblings allowed. That's good, and it's also good to touch base on a daily basis without a planned expedition. Ask your child to put down the video game occasionally and help you in the kitchen while you're making dinner. Or have him accompany you on errands. You'd be surprised how even adolescents crave this type of positive attention from parents. In fact, if you start this kind of communication and special time early, it is more likely that your child will want to continue the practice during the difficult adolescent years.

Build a foundation before the storm, and it will help you to weather the storm. To this end, additional resources have been provided in the appendix of this book that deal with challenging behaviors in gifted children.

Table 4.1. Parenting Strategies for Communicating with Gifted Children

- ✔ Offer young children limited choices.
- ✔ Gain buy-in from the child, if possible.
- ✔ Develop a problem-solving solution that:
  - o Describes the problem.
  - o Focuses on objectives.
  - o Develops and evaluates one or more specific solutions, with consequences and rewards.
- ✔ Spend time with the child outside of the difficult situation.

Afterword by Sarah

It seems that I was the obstinate child! Of course, I remember my younger self as a little angel, which would make all of the stories you've read falsehoods. But there are a lot of those stories, so I'm beginning to believe that my memory is selective. By the time I left home for college, many of the communication problems between my parents and me had been solved, leaving us better prepared for a functional adult relationship. However, one interaction threatened to set us back to those earlier communication problems.

When I was 20, I resolved to spend a summer in Israel. My mother strongly opposed this idea, fearing for my safety. At the start of our arguments, these worries were all rolled into one set of statements: "You're not going!" "It's too crazy!" "Why would you want to go someplace that dangerous?" "Why can't you just go to Europe, for heaven's sake?" My responses were equally inflammatory: "You can't stop me!" "You don't know anything about it!" "It's important to me!" "Why would I want to go to Europe?"

We took a step back and re-grouped. We quickly sorted out a few ideas. I was not asking my parents for money for the trip, and therefore I felt that I did not need their permission to go. However, they pointed out that they were paying for a large chunk of my college tuition. This argument made sense, and I agreed that unless I had their permission to go, I would not make the trip. Eventually, I composed a 10-page document, citing legitimate sources, which outlined safety concerns in Israel. It was so detailed that other students who wished to go requested copies in order to allay their own parents' fears. I was able to argue that, while frightening, terrorist bombings were extremely unlikely to affect any given individual. The time period when I was going was also during a deep lull in violence throughout all of Israel. In addition, I listed all of the precautions I would take in order to avoid what was already a small risk. For example, I promised never to take buses, as these were particular targets of terrorist attacks, and I would buy a temporary cell phone within a day of arriving so that I would never be out of contact. I'd like to think that my parents were so impressed with my logic that they let me go. Or maybe they were simply overwhelmed by my ferocity. In any case, I was able to go, but I was required to adhere to their rules while there. It was an inspirational trip—not only because of everything I saw and learned, but also because it was so self-motivated and independent. I'm certainly a more fearless, confident world traveler now because of it.

Part of what I take away from this story is that dealing with gifted children's spirit and will doesn't necessarily come easily or naturally; sometimes you have to consciously adhere to a reasonable set of guidelines. Doing so may temporarily make the child feel angry at not having her way. Ideally, however, those feelings give way to the eventual satisfaction of compromise and to stronger relationships.

I hope my Mom will back me up on this one, since I don't know the research, but I think we carry the communication styles we learn from our families into our other adult relationships. When my fiancé and I argue, we make a point of stopping if the discussion gets too heated and saying, "We're on the same team." We repeat this to each other as we calm ourselves down, and we can usually restart from a point of compromise after that. I wasn't sure when we started that pattern, but recently it became clear.

These days, of course, I rarely argue with my parents. However, planning a wedding brings out the worst (as well as the best) in all of us. I'm not sure how a bunch of normally sane people start caring so deeply about matching tuxedos and flower arrangements, but somehow this is the way of weddings. In the middle of a wedding-themed argument, my mother interrupted with, "Remember, we're on the same team, right?" So I suppose this is the communication style that I developed through disagreements with my parents and now consciously apply to other relationships. There are worse ways to get along.

CHAPTER 5

Why Don't You Make More Friends?

Understanding Socialization in Gifted Children

Friendship is born at that moment when one person says to another, "What! You too? I thought I was the only one."
~C. S. Lewis

I watched as my four-year-old daughter sat absorbed in a book while a crowd of excited children gathered around a birthday cake blazing with candles. As the other children in the room lined up to give presents to the birthday girl (one of our neighbor's children), I approached Jen.

"Honey, it's time for presents," I said.

"Okay," my daughter responded reluctantly, getting up but still clutching the book.

"Where did you get the book?" I asked.

"From home," she replied. "It's so good I can't put it down."

Although I was pleased that my daughter loved reading, I felt a pang of anguish. Jen seemed so removed and so focused on her own world, and I wondered—not for the first time—*Was this normal?*

Around me, little girls fluttered and laughed, bouncing up and down happily in their bright party dresses as they handed presents to the birthday girl, who ruled like a queen over the festivities. Nervously, I glanced back at my daughter, who was quietly absorbed again in the story unfolding in her hands. "Sweetie," I said, "why don't you put the book down and try to make some friends?" Sighing, she obeyed.

Little did I know that this would become an oft-repeated pattern with Jen. It went something like this. Understanding the need for social development, I would arrange for play dates or parties with other children her age. Smiling, she would agree and happily get into the car. When we arrived at our destination, she would dutifully go off to play, and I would leave to run errands. When I returned, however, Jen would often be ready to go, or sometimes she would be tucked into a corner, quietly reading a book and waiting for me. If the play date was at our house, I would make sure the children were all set and then disappear to another part of the house to do chores. Soon, the playmate would drift in to where I was, looking for companionship, and I would find Jen alone with a book, a puzzle, or a game.

This is not to say that Jen didn't have friends. In fact, my daughter always had, at every age, one or two very good and very intense friendships. Often, these were children with whom she shared an interest, such as reading or making up plays. I remember some outstanding theatrical performances starring my daughter and her friends, as well as many other happy times she enjoyed with playmates. But it took me a long time to realize that the best friendships were ones that *she* initiated, not ones I hoped for. I also realized, eventually, that if Jen made more friends, *I* would feel better—it would make *me* feel more popular. It had little to do with what was best for Jen—a humbling discovery.

Gifted Children's Need for Socialization

Research is mixed as to whether gifted students experience more social difficulties than other students.[33] It appears that young gifted children start out being socially accepted by their peers; however, problems often arise as they get older. In elementary school, the old myth about the gifted "nerd" being unpopular appears to be just that—a myth. Some research suggests that gifted elementary students are at least as well-liked as other students, if not more so,[34] and this happy state of affairs persists at least until the age of 13. Elementary gifted students even rate themselves as more socially popular than other students.[35]

However, the evidence that elementary gifted students are all socially popular is more nuanced. For example, in one study,[36] almost 500 students in grades 4-8 were asked to rate their peers on a variety of measures, including social popularity. In this study, 64 of the 500 students were identified as gifted and attended pull-out enrichment programs. Interestingly, gifted boys were rated highest by their peers in terms of popularity, while gifted girls were rated lowest. To complicate matters, gifted adolescents may express feelings of being "different," and they try various strategies to fit in. Gifted boys may mask their giftedness with humor, becoming the class clown.[37] Starting in middle school, gifted girls may mask their giftedness by performing poorly.[38] The higher the child's IQ, the more difficult time she may have adjusting to mainstream social situations.

Researchers have long understood that many gifted students prefer the company of older children, other gifted children, and adults.[39] This makes sense when you think about how we adults select friends. We don't choose friends on the basis of their age, but rather for their interests and abilities. For instance, if you are a 50-year-old who loves golf, you might like hanging out with a 30-year-old golfer because you share a passion and ability for golf that allows you to connect and enjoy each other's company. Similarly, if you are a 10-year-old child with an interest in and ability for mathematics, you might prefer to hang out with a 15-year-old who shares your interest and ability, rather than another 10-year-old who has no interest in math.

To complicate matters, gifted children may move through "play stages" more rapidly than other children.[40] Psychologists have identified developmental play stages through which children progress as they mature. If gifted children move through these stages more quickly than their non-gifted counterparts, friendships may be difficult, especially during adolescence when gifted children tend to look for levels of trust, fidelity, and authenticity that other children are not ready to provide.

So how do parents go about satisfying their child's very real need for socialization? It will help if you follow what I like to call the golden rule for children's socialization: *Let your child be your guide.* Before we get into this idea, though, we need to understand the differences between introverts and extroverts.

Introverts and Extroverts

Everyone lives life with an internal preference as to how they will deal with the outside world, and this preference appears to be programmed into us. People who derive pleasure from interacting with other people in the outside world are said to be extroverts. There are some specific characteristics of extroverts that make them easy to spot. They are usually people of action and achievement, making many friends wherever they go. They derive their energy from interacting with people, and so they feel energized when they do so. They learn by doing, and if left alone for too long, they may begin to feel uncomfortable.

On the other hand, people who live life in a world of ideas and who obtain their energy from being alone are said to be introverts. Introverts also have certain characteristics that make them easy to identify. They usually have a few close friends. They can concentrate intensely, and they tend to learn from observing. They are sometimes shy, and they often seek out opportunities to read or reflect quietly, alone.

These two personality types may be viewed as different ends of a continuum. We all sit somewhere along the continuum. Either way, our nature appears to be programmed into us, possibly genetically, from birth. We know that there are fewer introverts than extroverts in the general population, but among the gifted population, the reverse may be true—that is, there may be more introverts among gifted children (and adults) than extroverts.[41]

Society often tries to change introverts into extroverts, and many people view introversion as a condition to be cured. Traditionally, introverted children have been seen as too shy and lacking in social skills, so well-meaning teachers, guidance counselors, and parents have tried to expose them to opportunities for socialization. However, neither introversion nor extroversion is the "correct" way to be—they simply are tendencies with which we are born and which are very difficult to change. Indeed, when one considers how an introvert functions, trying to change him or her into an extrovert could be harmful. Like my daughter, Jen, many introverts refresh themselves with quiet solitude or with interactions with a limited number of trusted friends. At the end of a long day in which they've had to interact with the world, the last thing an introvert wants to do is socialize some more. Instead, this child may need some down time to read, draw, reflect, or simply dream.

It's not that introverted children or adults don't need friends; they do. However, the number of friendships they need may be far fewer than their extroverted friends and family need. Frequently, an introverted child may be happy with only one or two close friends, often ones of his own choosing. These friends may share interests and a sense of humor—they "get" each other's jokes, and they may also share abilities in one or more areas.

How do you know how many friends your child needs? It's important to keep in mind the "one is enough" rule—that is, most children need at least one friend to cherish, to play with, to laugh with, and with whom she feels comfortable. Beyond this friend, all bets are off, for many children are perfectly happy with only the one friend (although more extroverted children will probably want and even need additional friendships). If you let your child be your guide, you can't go wrong, for as long as she is happy and content, she's probably okay.

Each of my three children was different socially; they had different needs for friendships, both in terms of the numbers of friends each needed and also in terms of the types of friends they cultivated. As I've already stated, Jen was more introverted and rarely sought out friends. When she did make friends, she would make them one at a time. Sarah was more extroverted, and Josh was probably my most socially extroverted child. By the time Josh was in middle school, he had collected a whole group of friends, many of whom he still enjoys today.

I learned to listen to my children's conversations so that they could be my guide in this area. For example, if a child came to me on a rainy day with the mantra, "Mom, I'm bored," I didn't automatically assume it was socialization they were craving. Sometimes they just wanted my attention, and sometimes they needed an activity—a book or a game—to keep them occupied. I learned to watch their reactions when I suggested play dates with children. Did they appear eager to go? Did they push back? If they appeared reticent, I might suggest another friend. If that didn't work, I might abandon the idea altogether, suggesting an alternate activity.

Communicating with your child about his friendships is an important way of learning about them—whether the friendships are valuable to your child and how healthy they are. Take your cue from him. If he *loves, loves, loves* these friendships and appears to want more, you can encourage the parties and sleepovers. But it's also important to understand what he's getting from the friendships. Are these relationships healthy for him, or are they destructive? Do these friends encourage him to participate in unhealthy behavior, or are they identity-affirming?

Communication doesn't happen overnight. However, for me, the conversations about friendships frequently did happen at night, when my children and I were snuggling together and recounting the day. I always tried to approach the topics of friendships obliquely, using phrases such as, "Tell me about your new friend…" or "What do you think about…?" I tried to avoid using phrases such as, "Don't you love…?" or "I don't like…." Again, let your children be your guide as you explore how many and the types of friends they need.

What to Do if Your Child Is Unhappy Socially

If you truly sense that your child is having difficulty socially—she's unhappy with the number or quality of the friendships in her life—then there are several positive steps you can take to help. Dr. Sylvia Rimm[42] has developed some suggestions for handling these types of situations. First, it's extremely important that you develop and promote a harmonious family environment; your child will need the strength and support of her family during periods of social stress. Next, don't emphasize popularity and social success. Instead, explain to your child that social relationships often become easier to navigate after high school, and keep her focus on the future. Point out that as her peer group matures, she will be able to make friends more easily. Talk to her about how she will grow up to have many wonderful adventures in her life.

In the meantime, take advantage of your child's interests and abilities to enable him to make connections with other children who have similar interests and abilities. Many friendships are formed in clubs and other types of social groups, so make sure your child is involved in at least one or two after-school activities of his choosing that connect him with other children. Encourage sleepovers and other social events. Remember, though, that if your child is introverted, you may want to avoid inviting 10 children over, as it may overwhelm him. Instead, invite just one or two friends of his choosing. Make sure that your child has some social contact with other children, but don't think that every minute of every day after school must be filled with such social activity, for the goal here is for him to spend some time with other children while still allowing for the down time that many introverted children require.

It's important that the family be sensitive to the introverted child's needs as well. It's especially difficult for an introverted child if she is surrounded by extroverted family members, always talking, laughing, and trying to connect with her. Allowing her to experience some daily quiet down time will go a long way toward enabling her to connect with family members. Down time usually involves giving the child some peace and privacy—something an introvert values most highly.[43]

I remember when Jen, as a young teen, would disappear for hours into her room, searching for that quiet time to refresh herself. She would emerge later, responsive and communicative once again. I didn't understand her behavior at the time, but now, when I think about how she conducts her life as an adult, I still see the pattern of quiet down time followed by periods of socialization.

Children are different when it comes to their needs for socialization—some enjoy having many friends, and others are content with one or two. If you understand and respect your children for their uniqueness, as I eventually learned to do, they can be your guides on the matter of their friendships and social activities. By providing a nurturing, caring environment, you can help your children discover true and lasting friendships.

Table 5.1. Parenting Strategies to Help Gifted Children with Socialization

- ✔ Understand your child's need for socialization, and keep it apart from your own need for popularity.

- ✔ Understand where your child is on the introversion-extroversion continuum and the implications of this placement.

- ✔ Ensure that your child has at least one good friend.

- ✔ If your child is unhappy socially, arrange for get-togethers with one or two other children of his choosing.

- ✔ Make sure your child is involved with one or two clubs or other social groups of his choosing.

- ✔ Keep a harmonious family environment that can be a safe haven for your child during difficult times.

- ✔ Reassure your child that social relationships become easier as children grow older.

- ✔ Avoid pressuring your child to make more friends; let it happen naturally.

- ✔ Describe a bright future to your child that involves wonderful experiences.

Afterword by Jen

This chapter was a challenge for me, probably more so than the chapter on anxiety. I kept trying to write it and ending up unhappy with the results, so I talked to Mom about it while we were planning dinner one night. She told me that the difficulty I was having was part of the point of the chapter and that I should include it. So here goes.

My problem is that I'm not very emotionally invested in this topic. Of my mother's three children, I'm definitely the one who fits the introvert label the most, and the examples she uses to talk about socialization and friendships fit my situation, if only because Mom learned the most about her own issues through me. Mom and Dad figured out when I was still pretty young that I didn't need lots of friends and was perfectly happy doing my own thing. So any early attempts to push me to do something I wasn't interested in didn't result in much harm. More than that, though, I'm not very invested in the topic now because I wasn't then. I just didn't care enough.

This sounds strange, like I was some odd, detached child who never wanted anything to do with the people around her, and that's not quite right either. Like Mom said, I always had a few friends, and they were enough. The rest of it didn't bother me much. Maybe the best way to describe it is this: Most people seem to have strong feelings about their adolescent social lives. They were great! They were awful! High school was the best! High school was torture! I'm fewer than 10 years past my graduation, though, and I look back, not with longing or nausea, but with indifference. Perhaps a vaguely fond indifference, but still an indifference. I don't remember a lot of it. The memories have faded because, for me, there wasn't that much to them in the first place.

I realize that this sounds really horrible to some people, like I'm saying that my school, my acquaintances, and even some of my friends meant nothing. Of course that isn't true. The school was pretty good—better in some ways than in others—and it gave me a solid academic background that has served me well. My peers were about what you'd expect from a large group of teenagers—mostly undeveloped but with the potential that many of them are on their way to realizing. These people had—and have—tremendous value for the world in general and meaning for others in their lives. They just didn't play a very big role in my life.

I do have vivid memories of growing up. I remember the camping trailer my family bought for our cross-country road trips. I remember the notes my best friend and I passed during slow classes, the color of her ink, and the way we filled the pages with observations that seemed very deep at the time. I remember the heat of a light table as I leaned over it to tweak a newspaper layout. These memories stuck, so it's not like I just blurred out 18 years of my life. I think I remember them because they meant something to me at the time, in a way that interactions that have faded didn't. They still mean something. Some of our best family stories come from the trips we took in that camping trailer. My friend and I have conversations by phone now (we live several time zones apart). And although I haven't done a layout in years, I still judge the design of the magazines and newspapers I read. The point is that these things are what I remember most vividly. I didn't choose them; you don't get to do that. So there was nothing Mom could have done to make the friendships she wanted me to have more meaningful or more memorable. Those friendships she spent my early childhood pushing me to develop couldn't compare to the time I spent hanging out in the trailer or studying what I loved. They couldn't compare to the close friendships I *did* develop, although those were fewer in number. Because I learned to devote my time to the people and things that mattered to me, I was happy. Once Mom understood that, she was happier, too.

I'm still an introvert, although I've learned to see the value of casual socializing. (It got a lot easier when I stopped thinking I had to enjoy and be energized by it.) My family meets most of my social needs. But even with them, I need time alone. I have a small circle of friends, wonderful people all, so I'm not usually alone unless I want to be. I've found the less intense friendships of adulthood refreshing, though. They leave room for reflection and decompression, making them infinitely more enjoyable for an introvert. It has been one of the many pleasant surprises of growing up that these sorts of friendships are possible and that I may maintain as few or as many of them as I wish.

The moral of the story, as always, is that your child is in many ways essentially who he will always be. If he is an introvert, no amount of wishing—on his part or yours—will make him enjoy a very active social life. This doesn't mean that he can't be happy; it just means that his path will be a little different. I've actually found that the loneliest times of my life were periods when I was forcing myself to be very social. For one reason or another, I wasn't being honest with myself about what I needed, and that's far more destructive than not having "enough" friends could ever be. When I am honest with myself about who I am and what makes me happy, I usually spend time with fewer people but have more real friendships.

CHAPTER 6

No More Questions!

Dealing with Gifted Children's Insatiable Need to Know

The cure for boredom is curiosity.
There is no cure for curiosity.

~Dorothy Parker

In previous chapters, I've used examples of what not to say from the perspective of a parent. Another hat I've worn is that of a teacher of gifted students. Teaching gifted children is a little like being inside a nuclear reactor. Every minute of every school day in my gifted classroom, you could sense a pulse of energy coming from the children. From the minute I opened the door in the morning until the minute they left in the afternoon, the room was ablaze with questions and comments. I would no sooner walk through the door and plop my bag on the desk than students would surround me. "Mrs. H.," one student might cry out, "I discovered a tree frog in my backyard last night. What do tree frogs eat? Where do they come from?" Another would be jumping up and down to get my attention before blurting out, "Did you see the National Geographic special last night about the moon? I wonder why the moon doesn't go flying off into space?" A third student might be inspecting objects on my desk, focusing on a paperweight geode, asking, "What's that, and what is it made of?"

In addition to wanting to find out everything they could on many different topics of interest, my gifted students often liked to quiz me to determine how much *I* knew. For example, I once taught a fourth-grade boy who liked to bring in volumes of the encyclopedia. These were the days before widespread use of the Internet, so many children still had bound encyclopedias at home, and this student had made it his personal ambition to read through the entire set. He was at that time on the third volume (C) and wanted to chat about everything he read. "Mrs. H.," he might say," do you know what state Charleston is in?" Or he might swagger up to my desk and peer at me before quizzing, "Where do pickles come from?"

I diligently answered him if I knew the answers, but sometimes (okay, maybe frequently), I didn't know the answers, and I quickly learned not to bluff. Once he asked me where Cypress was, and not being totally up on my geography, I tried to fake an answer. "Is it in the Pacific?" I asked. "Ha! No!" he cried triumphantly. "It's an island in the Eastern Mediterranean." "Hmmm…" I replied, humbled.

If you are a parent of a gifted child, you may know exactly what I'm talking about. As both a teacher and parent, I eventually learned how to deal with my students' constant questioning, as well as their growing awareness that I didn't know everything.

Dealing with Constant Questioning

When I first started teaching, I would go home and prepare careful lesson plans for the next day or the next week and do my best to stick to them. I liked everything nice and neat, and you could set your clock by how carefully I timed my curricular units. Unfortunately, that approach didn't leave any time for children's questions, and boy were there questions! Questions came from almost every single child in the classroom—sometimes multiple questions from one child—and often simultaneously. It seemed as if every school day consisted almost entirely of "Why?" and "How?" and "When?" How was I supposed to think, much less deliver lessons?

At first, I tried a two-pronged, proactive approach. First, I ignored most of the questions. Second, for the questions I did answer, I glared at the offending student if she asked a second question or if she blurted out the question without first raising a hand. If you've never taught in a classroom, this approach might seem a little harsh, and maybe it was, but we were talking about survival here. I had a preconceived idea of the perfect classroom—all students seated quietly, hands folded, paying attention, and hanging on my every word—and this is what I was after. But still, the questions kept coming.

It wasn't until I understood the nature of giftedness that I realized that the questions weren't going to stop, and I learned how to deal with the "problem." In fact, it really wasn't until I understood that the questions weren't a problem, but rather an opportunity to *teach*, that I effectively managed the situation. I can't say that it was one particular student who taught me this, but more likely years of students gathering at my desk, their eyes alight with curiosity, their questions pouring out, that drove home the point that the questions were actually desirable. After all, wasn't that what I was there for—to teach? Isn't that the purpose of schools—to ignite a desire for learning? Here I had students who were asking, even begging, to learn, and I was annoyed. What if I instead saw the situation as an opportunity?

As I took a good hard look at the situation, I discovered that I wasn't annoyed by the questions, but rather the constant demands of the students—demands that I couldn't always fulfill. Because I did have to cover certain subjects during the course of a day, I couldn't keep interrupting my lessons to deal with questions. I realized that the trick was to find a way to answer students' questions while at the same time keeping the classroom momentum going.

At first, I developed tricks and devices designed to delay students' questions until I could deal with them. I made a "Question Hat" that was topped with a big question mark, and I told students that when I put the hat on, they could feel free to interrupt me with questions and comments. If the hat was off, they should wait. I worked diligently with the students on raising their hands instead of simply shouting out their questions and ideas, and soon I had a modicum of control in the classroom. I was then able to develop deeper and more meaningful techniques that not only helped me establish control in the classroom, but also encouraged students' curiosity and exploration. I developed classroom surveys to determine students' interests. I brought in learning materials and made centers that tied into those interests.

Admitting that You Don't Know Everything

The hardest lesson that I had to learn, both as a parent and as a teacher, may have been that it's okay to let children know that you don't know everything. Young children look to the adults in their lives for answers, and as parents and teachers, we want to be able to provide them. After all, we would like to think that we are good information providers. However, two problems arise when we lead children to believe that we are ultimate authorities on everything:

1. We really *don't* know everything, and children will find out sooner or later that we are bluffing.

2. When we readily provide children with the answers to everything, we discourage them from developing what I like to call their "finding out" skills—the skills they need to know to locate information, to access the information, and to make sense of the information.

I told my students that I was a learner as well, and I didn't pretend to have all of the answers when they asked me questions. Always, though, I respected the question, and if I didn't know the answer, I encouraged or enabled them to find out. Sometimes we stopped everything and found out together.

Why Gifted Children Ask so Many Questions

Why do many gifted children ask an inordinate amount of questions? What is behind their insatiable need to know? Dabrowski[44] included intellectual overexcitability in his research, which is the desire on the part of the child to explore his or her environment and the world of ideas. Often, this exploration takes the form of reading or questioning. Researchers aren't quite sure why this trait applies to so many gifted children; however, it seems clear that for many of these children, the need to know feels as vital as the need to breathe. Although a gifted child's curiosity and need to know are sometimes exhilarating, they can also be exasperating. Consider the following conversation that might take place between a mother and her son or daughter as they are driving in the car:

Mother:	Look! A rainbow!
Child:	What's a rainbow made out of?
Mother:	Tiny droplets of water…
Child:	How do they get up in the sky?
Mother:	(Concentrating on the question, mother presses the gas pedal a little harder than she should.) They evaporate up into the sky.
Child:	How do they evaporate up into the sky?
Mother:	It happens when the sun shines on water and provides energy.
Child:	What's energy?
Mother:	(Distracted by the question and how to answer it, mother shoots past her exit on the highway. Sighs.) I'm not really sure how to explain it. (Looks for the nearest ramp to the next exit so that she can turn around.)
Child:	Why not?
Mother:	Energy is like something that you get from food.
Child:	So the sun gives food to the water and that makes it go up to make a rainbow?
Mother:	(Overshoots her exit again.) Sigh.

Certainly we want to encourage our children to thirst for knowledge, but there is a time and a place for conversations filled with questions. I like to think that, as parents and teachers, we're developing "academic explorers," or children who will go out and explore the world, asking questions and thinking critically about issues. However, I'm enough of a realist to understand that not everyone can drop everything they're doing and answer every question the moment it arises.

So how do you deal with your youngster's curiosity in a way that allows you to remain sane without discouraging your child from asking questions? You can honor and respect the child's intellectual curiosity but delay answering certain questions until you are able to give them your full attention. One system I have used is to designate a "parking lot," which is a physical area where questions may be "parked" until a time when they can be discussed. This area may be large, such as a whiteboard, or it may be small, such as a binder or small journal. Any surface on which questions can be recorded will suffice. The important idea is that not only do you record the question, but you also set aside a time and a place to address the question. It's okay to forget occasionally, but questions do need to be addressed. Let's replay the previous conversation, only now we'll include a reference to the "parking lot."

> Mother: Look! A rainbow!
>
> Child: What's a rainbow made out of?
>
> Mother: Tiny droplets of water...
>
> Child: How do they get up in the sky?
>
> Mother: They evaporate up into the sky.
>
> Child: How do they evaporate up into the sky?
>
> Mother: It happens when the sun shines on water and provides energy.
>
> Child: What's energy?

Mother: I'm not really sure how to explain this right now. Energy is a complex thing. Why don't we put this question in the "parking lot," and when we get home, we'll look it up together after dinner.

Child: Okay, I like that idea.

Mother: Here's the "parking lot" for questions. (She pulls a small journal from the glove compartment and hands it to the child.) Can you write the question down, since I'm driving?

Child: Sure! Hey, there's another question in here from last time. Can we look both of them up?

Mother: Okay, no problem!

It's important to admit to your children when you don't know something and encourage them to learn it along with you.[45] Little children tend to look up to their parents and admire them as all-knowing gods and goddesses, and parents are sometimes unwilling to let this go. However, it's important that as they age, your children begin to see you more realistically. After all, let's be honest and admit that there are many things that we adults do not know, and it's not so bad that children understand this, for a number of reasons.

First, sharing your lack of knowledge says to the child, "I'm not perfect, and I don't expect you to be either." Because gifted children frequently deal with perfectionism (see Chapter 1), letting them know that the adults in their lives are not perfect sends the message that they don't have to strive for this unattainable goal. Next, helping children understand that you don't know something but are willing to learn imparts a valuable message about learning—that learning is a lifelong pursuit, and one never reaches the end of learning. Finally, by saying to the child that you are willing to participate in his experiences as a partner in learning, you are demonstrating that you value learning and, perhaps even more importantly, you value your child's learning. You are showing him that, although you are busy, you are willing to take time from your activities to focus on his learning opportunities. If it is true that children come to value what we as parents value, then it is also true that with this approach, your children will come to value learning.

Finding Information to Answer the Questions

What are some approaches you might use to find out the answers to your child's questions? Fortunately, with the rapid progression of technology, finding answers has becoming increasingly easier. Sometimes answers are as close as a few keystrokes entered into a search engine like Google. I think about how much harder this exercise was a few decades ago, before the advent of the Internet. Today, details on everything from *aardvarks* to *zoology* and more are at our fingertips. However, a more difficult question for adults now is: How do we locate information about our children's questions that is both age-appropriate and simple enough for them to understand? And how can we teach our children to become more independent and sophisticated consumers of information?

Of course, one of the many ways to find answers is to take a trip to the local library. I highly recommend occasionally doing this with your child because it introduces her to the world of books. You may wish to consult with the local librarian, introducing your child to him. A "guide on the side" is absolutely critical as you begin to explore the wealth of options now available to you for obtaining information. Walking into a library with a parent can be an experience that a child will always remember. There's nothing that can substitute for the tangible book—its heft and its distinct smell—and many of us have pleasurable memories associated with books.

However, it is only realistic to recognize that much of the information you'll be locating today with your child will be digital, online. And rather than allowing a young child to search for this information on her own, wise parents will sit with her as she explores the answers to her questions. There are three reasons to do so. First, as I've mentioned before, it sends the message that the questions are important to you. If you're taking your valuable time to focus on developing your child's intellectual curiosity, you're demonstrating that curiosity is valuable because you're curious, too. Curiosity is a powerful tool because it is at the root of all learning and can foster a lifelong love for intellectualism.

Second, your presence is a safety barrier that provides protection in an unsafe environment. I'm not going to dwell on the dangers of the Internet because I believe that most parents understand them. They're real, and they should not be overlooked. It is estimated that as of 2011, the Internet contains approximately 155 million websites,[46] many of them unregulated. This means that many sites contain information that is unrestricted, unreliable, and sometimes even harmful to children. As such, it has become especially important for children to become *information literate*—to learn how to efficiently locate appropriate information and then evaluate that information once they do so.[47] Gifted children may be in an especially vulnerable position because they are often able to locate sophisticated information and are capable of reading it, but they may not be capable of dealing with it emotionally.

The third reason that you should be physically present when your child explores the answers to his questions is that you can help him locate and evaluate information—no small feat in today's online environment. Many times, a child will search for information on a general topic such as "anteaters" and find himself immersed in a world of graduate theses on anteaters, professor's published papers on anteaters, and even ways to purchase videos about anteaters. How is an elementary (or even a middle school) child to know how to sift through all of the information to find what he needs?

Table 6.1. Search Engines for Children*

Name of Search Engine Description	URL
Ask for Kids (formerly Ask Jeeves for Kids)	
Children enter a question using natural language, and the engine searches multiple databases until it locates sites with potential answers. The engine also checks for appropriateness. Sites have been selected by an editor.	www.askforkids.com

Name of Search Engine Description	URL
Awesome Library	
Designed for students in grades K-12 and their teachers and parents, this engine provides access to more than 35,000 safe websites.	www.awesomelibrary.org
iPL2 for Kids	
A fairly new site, iPL2 is the result of a merger of the Internet Public Library (IPL) and the Librarians' Internet Index (LII). Older students may benefit especially from access to use of premiere sites such as the Library of Congress, National Science Foundation, and Smithsonian Institution.[51]	www.ipl.org/div/kidspace/index.html
KidsClick	
This engine is suited for children in grades 4-9. It currently searches approximately 6,400 high-quality sites. The site is run by the School of Library and Information Science at San Jose University.	www.kidsclick.org
KOL Homework Help, Jr.	
This is a directory of online resources for students in grades K-2.	http://kids.aol.com/homework-help/junior
TeKMom's Search Tools for Students	
This site brings together a number of safe search engines for children.	www.tekmom.com/search
Yahoo! Kids (formerly Yahooligans)	
This engine searches for appropriate sites for children ages 7-12. It is the oldest major search engine for children. Sites are handpicked by Yahoo staff for appropriateness.	http://kids.yahoo.com

* These search engines were current at the time of publication of this book.

As a parent, you can teach your child how to navigate through this mountain of information with a few simple steps:

1. Teach your child to locate information by using some simple, age-appropriate search engines. There are some decent search engines on the market today that screen websites

and only select ones that are age-appropriate and content-appropriate. See Table 6.1 for a listing of these sites.

2. Utilize filters. Users have the ability to turn on filters in most major search engines (such as Google and Yahoo) that will make content safer for little ones. For example, in Google, filters may be set to "Strict," "Moderate," or "No Filtering" to screen out inappropriate content.

3. Teach your child *how* to search for information. There is an art to searching for information on the Internet, and search terms do matter. Consider, for example, if you wanted to search for information on moon landings. If you use the search term "moon," you might come up with many websites about physical features of the moon, a video about the moon, a moon phase calculator, a website about Moon Township, Pennsylvania, and more. If, however, you search for "lunar landing 1969," you are much more likely to find the information you need. Teach your child to be specific in her searches. It is important to use correct spelling. Place exact phrases in quotes ("moon landing," not moon landing). Boolean logic may help as well.[48] Use the word *and* when you want to see only sites that combine two or more keywords. Use *or* when you want to see sites that contain either keyword. For example, the search terms *moon and phases* will return different websites than *moon or phases*. The first search is likely to return websites related to the topic of moon phases, and the second will return websites about the moon (some of which will contain information about phases) and other sites about phases of human development, phases of mitosis, and more.

4. Teach your child how to utilize resources other than routine search engines. Gifted children sometimes have a need to investigate sophisticated resources, and fortunately, there is a wealth of information available beyond the standard search engines. Many states have their own digital libraries

that may be accessed online and utilized free of charge with a public library card.[49] To determine whether your state maintains a digital library, Google your state's name and the words *digital library*.

5.   Teach your child how to evaluate whether or not the information looks accurate. Children (and adults) may believe that because something is "written" on the Internet, it's true. Consider, though, a recent study in which researchers created a fake website about a fictitious "tree octopus" and asked seventh graders from middle schools across the state to review it and rate its credibility.[50] In a troubling finding, all but one of the students rated the site as "very credible." (You can see the tree octopus site at http://zapatopi.net/treeoctopus.) Now granted, the site looks real, but what does it mean when students can't tell the real apart from the fake, the serious apart from the absurd? It means that parents and teachers need to instruct children on how to evaluate websites for validity and accuracy.

One way to start teaching your child how to evaluate information on the Internet is to look at sources. If there is an "About Us" link on the site's home page, teach your child how to click on it and examine the site for information. If the website is a personal web page, for example, the information might be less reliable that a research corporation's web page. Also teach your child how to look carefully for examples of biased statements that might tip him off to the idea that the facts could be compromised. For example, if the website touts a medical cure for diabetes and it: (1) provides no evidence of clinical studies, and (2) tries to sell the cure for an outrageous price, you'll want to point these facts out to your child. As adults, most of us have learned to be skeptical of these types of come-ons, and for good reason, but children have been taught to respect authority and also to respect the written word, and so they might be more susceptible to these and other less obvious scams. For a more complete list of ways to evaluate websites, refer to Table 6.2.

Table 6.2. Checklist for Evaluating Websites

- ✔ Can you determine who the authors are? Do they provide their credentials?

- ✔ Can you tell what the purpose is?

- ✔ Is the information that is provided clear?

- ✔ Is the information objective or subjective?

- ✔ Does the author present two sides of an argument?

- ✔ Is information supported, and are sources provided for the support?

- ✔ Is there contact information?

- ✔ When was the website last updated?

- ✔ Does the website appear well-designed? Are the pictures clear? Is the website easy to read and navigate? Do the links work?

In conclusion, it's important that you view your child's constant questioning as an opportunity rather than a nuisance. Understand that the questioning is an opportunity to spend more time with your child, during which you will help her develop into an "academic explorer" with a lifelong love of learning. In the meantime, you'll become closer as you spend more quality time together. In 20 years, when your child has children asking questions of their own, she may turn to you and say, "Remember all those questions I used to ask? How did you put up with it?" Smiling, you'll look deeply into her eyes, struggling to see the little girl that she used to be. You'll reply, "It was always a joy." And you'll mean it.

Table 6.3. Parenting Strategies to Deal with Gifted Children's Constant Questioning

✔ Understand your child's need for information, and try to view it as a positive trait.

✔ Establish a system, such as a "parking lot," in which questions are placed until you can deal with them.

✔ Take your child to the library occasionally.

✔ Let your child know that you value her questions by sitting down at an appointed time to discuss them.

✔ Teach your child about online safety.

✔ Show your child how to use some age-appropriate search engines.

✔ Help your child learn how to evaluate websites for accuracy.

Author note: I did not ask one of my children to write an afterword for this chapter, as this issue was not a serious concern in our home.

CHAPTER 7

If You Don't Get Your Grades Up, No More Dance Lessons!

Motivating Your Gifted Child through Selective Achievement

I am always doing that which I cannot do, in order that I may learn how to do it.

~Pablo Picasso

Many parents, at one time or another, have threatened to take away the one thing that our children love in order to motivate them to improve their grades. Unfortunately, when we do this, we may be taking away the one thing that validates them. A tale about Josh will illustrate the power and influence of a positive interest or passion in a child's life.

One afternoon, I entered the den and found my son, Josh, asleep on the couch, a habit that had become ingrained since he started high school. What to do? Normally, I would have bypassed my sleeping son, only waking him up to call him in to dinner. This time, I decided to try a different strategy. "Josh," I whispered, standing over him and shaking him slightly, "wake up!" He didn't move, so I shook a little harder. Slowly, my 6'4" son's eyes opened and stared at me. "What?" he complained, annoyed at having been awakened.

"Why are you sleeping on a school day?" I asked.

"What do you mean? I always nap when I come home," was his reply.

"That's my point," I said. "When there are so many things going on after school, why would you want to sleep the whole afternoon?"

Suspiciously, my son looked at me. "Like what?" he grumbled.

"Well…like sports or yearbook or service groups," I answered.

He rolled his eyes. "You could visit the patients at a nursing home." I glanced at him hopefully. Once again, I saw the eye-roll.

At this point I had a choice. I could, as I had done in the past, walk away and do nothing. I could also have said, "If you don't get your grades up, I'm going to take away your bike." This approach had also been previously used and had failed. Finally, I decided on a new approach. "Look," I said, my voice becoming slightly more on edge, "I can tell that nothing I've mentioned appeals to you. But I also think that it's important for you to get off the couch and get involved in something constructive—anything. It can be your choice. But you *are* going to pick one thing and see it through. I will take you to whatever activity you choose and bring you home, but you are going to do something besides lie on this couch."

Now my son began to look panicked. "What if I don't like it?" he asked.

"Then you don't have to continue with it," I bargained. "But you are going to try one thing and stick with it until it ends." My son looked at me suspiciously, and I could tell that he was evaluating what I had just said and the possible outcomes. Questions were obviously rolling around in his head: Did I mean it? Was there a way around it? What if he was miserable? What could he choose that would cause him the least amount of pain?

Suddenly, he said, "The drama club is putting on a play, and I know some of the people in the cast. I won't try out for a part, but I'll work backstage during the play." Immediately, my eyes lit up. "Deal!" I replied, and we shook on it.

I'm not quite sure what was in my son's mind when he shook my hand that day, but that moment proved to be a turning point for Josh. I picked him up at school a couple of weeks later, and he announced casually that he had signed up for some backstage work for the new play.

"Great!" was my enthusiastic reply. "When are rehearsals?"

"For the next six weeks, almost every afternoon," he answered, watching for my reaction. I tried not to show surprise as I realized I would be picking him up for six weeks after school instead of letting him ride home on the bus or in the car with his older sister, who drove to and from school. I turned away thinking it was worth it.

For the next six weeks, true to his word, Josh went to every rehearsal and learned backstage crafts such as lighting, makeup, set design, and more. I kept talking to him and encouraging him. "What's it like?" I would query as he plopped into the seat next to me in the car. "What did you get to do today?" And we would chat about how he was learning how to work the lights or build a set. "Remember," I would say when he seemed tired or lagging, "it's only for six weeks." He was silent.

Six weeks flew by, and soon it was time for the show. Josh's father and I attended on opening night. Even though we wouldn't see our son, we wanted him to know that we were there in the audience and that we supported him. As we watched the actors perform onstage, we admired the details in the set design and lighting. We recalled the little stories that Josh had told us about the preparation for the performance. We felt connected with our son.

That night, as we drove home, I turned to Josh in the backseat of the car. "Well, you've fulfilled your end of the bargain," I noted. "Tomorrow, I suppose you can go back to sleeping on the sofa."

"Actually, Mom," Josh replied," the drama club is performing *The Wizard of Oz* next, and I thought I might try out for a small part." There was a long silence in the car.

"I think that could be arranged," I smiled.

Josh tried out for *The Wizard of Oz* and landed a small part as a winged monkey. He cavorted with the best of the winged monkeys on and offstage, and in the meantime started making more friends with the students in the drama troupe. The next show was *Beauty and the Beast*, and Josh was determined that he should land a singing role. I was surprised, as he had never expressed an interest in singing before. Evidently, he was surprised, too, because he turned to me and said, "I can't sing, but I do want to play Gaston." Gaston is one of the lead roles in the play, and we knew it was a stretch for Josh.

"Well," I replied, "why don't we get you voice lessons for a few weeks and see what happens?" After doing so, Josh tried out, and although he didn't get the role of Gaston, he was able to perform in a minor singing role (the secondary villain). Interestingly, the director of the school's chorus, which was called OPUS, took a liking to my son's voice during the rehearsal process. OPUS wasn't an ordinary group—its members sang at competitions all over the country and usually won. It was well-known and well-respected for its outstanding vocal arrangements, especially of classical voice pieces. The director approached Josh and asked him to try out for OPUS, and a few weeks later, he did. You can guess the rest—he successfully auditioned and was accepted into OPUS. Now Josh was involved with two groups—drama and OPUS—and he continued with those associations throughout high school. He acted in increasingly larger parts in plays, eventually going on to play Atticus Finch in *To Kill a Mockingbird*. He flew to London and San Francisco to perform with OPUS. His best friends in high school came from those two groups.

My son no longer had time to lie on the couch after school. He was productive and busy, and the interesting thing is that the busier he became, the more he was able to accomplish. Many days he worked 16 to 18 hours (including classes and after-school activities), an occurrence that repeated itself so frequently that I became concerned he wasn't getting enough sleep. When this level of productivity occurred, I marveled at how much time and energy he was willing to invest in projects for which he held a deep and abiding interest.

Selective Achievement

If you have a child regularly sleeping on the couch, you need to do some diagnostic work. Your child may be unmotivated or bored, or she may be depressed. If she's depressed, she probably won't appear animated very often, if ever. She may have difficulty sleeping, and she may lose her appetite. She could have trouble concentrating in school, and she might even lose interest in activities she once loved. Depression is very different from what I'm about to describe, and if you believe that your child may be depressed, there are resources listed in the appendix to help you.

However, if your child is focused and animated when she's involved with an activity in which she's interested, she may not be depressed. She may stay out late to complete the activity, and she may talk for days on end about nothing else. You may wonder why she doesn't place the same importance on her studies (where her grades may be lackluster), and she may invest very little time in preparing for projects and examinations. I can sum up the situation with this type of child in two words: *selective achievement.*

In Chapter 2, I introduced the concept of underachievement, in which a child doesn't perform at the level at which he is capable. We know that the causes of underachievement differ from child to child and often are related to a variety of factors. Individual factors such as personality play a role, as do school-related factors such as inappropriate curriculum. Home-related factors such as family stress, or social factors such as lack of acceptance by a peer group may also influence underachievement. Frequently, an underachiever is a child who doesn't do his homework or study for tests. He's usually involved in few or no extracurricular activities, and he may be psychologically at risk for low self-esteem, depression, and more.

An underachiever and a selective achiever differ in several ways. An underachiever usually fails to live up to his academic potential because of some type of problem—the curriculum may be too challenging, he may have a skills deficit or a learning disability, or he may be experiencing some type of problem at home—to name only a few. A selective achiever is usually quite capable, and when properly motivated, he will work extremely hard at tasks that he loves. On the surface, these two children might look the same, but they each require different approaches from the concerned adults in their lives. The underachiever, as we discussed in Chapter 2, needs caring teachers and adults to diagnose the root causes of his underachievement and then act to remedy them. The selective achiever needs to be motivated to accomplish something positive and then (eventually) to learn that motivation and accomplishment bring their own rewards.

Achievement and Society

The notion of selective achievement calls into question our achievement-oriented value system, especially here in the United States. Many of our children, especially our gifted children, are trained from a very young age to achieve. Parents start as early as in the womb, eagerly holding IPods playing "Baby Mozart" next to Mom's tummy so that the brain cells of the developing fetus may be stimulated. Many children, especially in large cities, are on waiting lists for the most prestigious schools from birth and then spend the first few years of their lives prepping for the kindergarten entrance "examination." Incredibly, I recently read an article in *The New York Times Magazine*[52] in which parents paid for answers to these early examinations, largely consisting of IQ tests, so that their children could be trained to achieve higher scores and be admitted into the school of the parents' choice.

The pressure to achieve doesn't stop when children enter school. Bright students are pushed by well-meaning parents to achieve at increasingly higher levels, first in primary and later in the prestigious secondary academies. Usually, the goal of all of this is to gain admission into the top Ivy League schools, where the pressure to achieve continues. Even in areas of the country that that don't routinely emphasize this particularly elite path to education, the pressure is there, and it's real. As a teacher of the gifted, I can't tell you how many times I sat through parent-teacher conferences that went something like this:

Teacher:	Your daughter is very strong academically.
Parent:	Thank you. But you know, I don't think she's pushing herself hard enough.
Teacher:	But she has an "A" average in my class now. She pays attention in class, she always turns in her homework, and she's a happy, well-adjusted girl.
Parent:	Yes, but she should have an A+. Is there any additional work you could provide her that would bring her grade up?

It is important that we as parents recognize that some pushes for achievement may be over the top. Two questions to ask yourself if you find that your child is having difficulty are whether your wish for your child to earn better grades is: (1) reasonable, and (2) possible. Some of you may raise your eyebrows at both of these considerations. After all, we are used to thinking of our children as limitless and multi-talented, and there is a belief in our society that if one only works hard enough, every goal is achievable. However, this assumption fails to consider that children are unique and have different strengths and weaknesses.

If your child is earning a B+ or an A in mathematics, it could be that she is already pushing herself, and to push beyond this limit is neither reasonable nor possible. It could also be that your child sees no additional benefit to putting more time into mathematics due to a lack of interest in math or a stronger interest in another subject. Perhaps she is using the extra two hours that it would require each week to increase her grade in mathematics to an A+ to plan the next great American novel. Indeed, countless writers, scientific thinkers, and innovators from Shakespeare to Einstein were scolded for daydreaming in class. If your child is neither interested in nor capable of attaining perfect grades, why push her? Why not let her enjoy her childhood to some degree? Parents must eventually step back, take a breath, and relax, trusting in the understanding that if a child gets a few B's, it won't ruin her chances for a happy life.

Also, if we parents are honest, we recognize that no one (not even ourselves) performs at peak efficiency 100% of the time. We all have jobs that we love to do and others that we hate and will put off as long as possible. For me, the tasks I love and those I hate used to create a constant inner conflict. I love writing, and I hate housework. But I was raised in an immaculate home where you could eat off the floor, and it was an embarrassment to my mother if anyone saw dust under a sofa or grime on the lid of a pot. It has taken me years to accept that it's okay to neglect housework in favor of writing—the thing I love. I am finally able to say with confidence that I believe that no one should look under a sofa in the first place, and grime on the lid of the pot is evidence of the fact that the person in charge of the kitchen loves to cook. On the other hand, I have always been able to sit and write for hours, or research articles, books, and lesson plans for my students. Some of the happiest days I have spent were sitting in front of a fire on a cold winter's day, happily typing at my computer, household dust gradually piling up around me.

Some people dislike certain tasks but do them anyway. Others, adults and children alike, do what they love and put off tasks they don't like for as long as possible. For adults, this situation usually isn't disastrous because adults are not evaluated on each and every task. No one, except possibly my husband, cares whether the house is clean or not. However, unfortunately for children, schools do evaluate children's tasks and their task commitment almost continuously in the form of test scores and grades. Tasks that students would rather not do often result in poor grades. Sometimes the student is sufficiently talented that the poor grades are B's or C's, but sometimes the situation is worse, and the student's grades plummet to D's and F's. Many parents become concerned with B's and C's, sensing that their children are capable of doing better, and most parents are completely baffled by D's and F's, particularly when they see their children putting forth great effort in areas that they enjoy.

Motivating Selective Achievers

How do we motivate our selective achievers? It's not a simple question, and it's not a simple task, for each child is unique in terms of his or her interests and abilities. The first important step is to find out about your child's interests. You may fall into the trap of thinking that you know them already. However, many interests lie dormant, as did Josh's, until you find the right activity to draw them out. After-school clubs, competitions, sports, volunteer work, and other activities may prove invaluable. Encourage your child to sample some of these, and let him be your guide. Don't dominate him or insist that he try one particular activity, for he may turn out to hate it and then blame you, which will be entirely counter-productive. Instead, question him about what he may find exciting or interesting, and then develop an agreement with him that he will try one or two activities. This way, he will feel like the choice is his own and will be more likely to enjoy the activities. Be specific in your agreement about which activity or activities he will try and for how long. If you aren't lucky and don't find the activity that "clicks" the first time, keep trying. Schools and communities are filled with enrichment programs and activities. A list of several ideas and resources is included in the appendix of this book.

Once your child has found an activity that motivates him, insist that he continue with the activity until a logical stopping point. You may have to keep his initial involvement short, as I did by requiring Josh to be involved with only one play, because it may be easier to motivate your child if he thinks that all he has to do is commit for a limited amount of time. Often, however, this short period of time is enough to motivate the child to go further, especially if the activity is enjoyable and there are children his own age that are open and welcoming in the group. If, however, your child finds that he doesn't want to continue with the activity after his involvement is over, don't push. Perhaps the activity or the setting wasn't right for him. It's important that you honor your child's feelings and any agreements that you made with him when you were convincing him to do the activity. That way, your child will come to understand that you trust him to evaluate when something's good for him and when it's not, and you will honor your word. Don't give up, however. Insist that he try something else and follow through in the same manner.

Don't Take Away Your Child's Interests

When your child finds a pleasurable activity, allow her to continue her involvement with it. Never cut it off by saying, "If your grades don't improve, I'm going to take [insert the thing she loves here] away from you!" Sometimes, the thing that she loves is the only thing that's holding her together. It may be that she's the soccer star and that on the soccer field (and only on the soccer field), she gets to shine. In the classroom, she may be unmotivated and sloppy, but on the soccer field, she knows that she can accomplish her dreams. Why would you take that away? It probably won't bring her grades up, and it will have two ill effects: (1) it will turn her against you because you took away the one thing she loves, and (2) it may very well send the message that she shouldn't try to become proficient at anything because it will be taken away.

Instead, you have to be clever. Begin by talking with your child about how much she loves the activity and why. Discuss how she feels when she does the activity, as well as her level of involvement. Say things such as, "I notice that you've been getting better at soccer. Your drop kick is so much more skilled than when you began, and your teammates all seem to want you to play offense. Why is that?" Slowly, your child will begin to open up to you, telling you of her hopes, her dreams, her wins, and her losses. This new communication may build bridges that you can then apply to other areas. You might eventually say, "It feels good to win there, doesn't it? You know why you win so much? It's because you practice hard, and you work at becoming better." Don't try to apply it to the classroom—she'll eventually make the connection herself and learn that hard work results in improvement.

You child may never be a star in the classroom, for she may not possess the specific skill set (e.g., organizational and self-regulation skills), but this approach will probably spill over so that she will at least maintain her grades until she gets to college, at which time she may focus on something she loves. Plus (and this may be the most important thing of all), she may have carved out a sense of identity—a sense that she has a niche and is good at something—that will carry her through the rest of her academic career and beyond. Self-efficacy, or the belief that we are capable of doing something, is a powerful motivator, and research[53] suggests that with it, we persist when the going gets tough because we believe that we can get through it, and perhaps because we believe that over time, we may accomplish our dreams.

Table 7.1. Parenting Strategies to Deal with Selective Achievement in Gifted Children

- ✔ Evaluate your desire to have your child "succeed." Is it: (1) within the realm of possibility, and (2) reasonable?

- ✔ Question your child on his interests. What classes and activities would he find most interesting?

- ✔ Insist that your child become involved with one or two classes or activities that he really likes.

- ✔ Insist that your child see the activity through for a predetermined period.

- ✔ If the first activity doesn't do the job, keep trying!

- ✔ Once your child has found an activity he likes, support it.

- ✔ Discuss with your child:
  - o Why he likes the activity (be specific)
  - o How he feels when he does the activity
  - o The benefits of the activity
  - o How he's improving in the activity
  - o How the improvement is linked to effort

Afterword by Josh

This chapter is much easier for me to write about, for obvious reasons—it paints me in a much better light. Let's say for these purposes that underachievement is not my best color. But *selective achievement*, now there's a label I can get behind. Mom was correct that I was spending too much time on that couch. As I came to find out later, the activities that eventually took me away from my afternoon siestas turned out to be some of my most fulfilling experiences during high school. The friends that I made and the lessons I learned are still very much a part of my life today.

The fact of the matter is that I did struggle with underachievement as a young teenager. But looking back at the choices I made later in high school, I realize that I was really a selective achiever. I loved and still love every second of working in the arts, whether it is lighting design or arranging a piece of music. As I mentioned in Chapter 2, just because I didn't apply myself to American history doesn't mean I couldn't do the work. I just didn't see the merit of putting in the extra time in the subjects I didn't appreciate. As I started participating in things that did interest me, I had no issues with giving myself over completely to that particular activity.

Teenagers are constantly struggling to find somewhere to fit in, to be the best at something, or to feel like they are contributing to something. Some kids find their niche in sports, some make friends easily and find a sense of belonging in their circle of friends, and some, like myself, find their place in activities like drama or music. This isn't to say that these kinds of typical high school activities are the only ways in which a child can be happy, but these are the things that I believe helped push me and all of my peers through some tough years when our skin wasn't quite so clear.

The story my mom tells about me lounging on the couch is true. I wasn't bored exactly; I just didn't know where to spend my time. I hadn't found something I needed that also needed me. After deciding not to continue playing in the symphonic band (I played a pretty mean trombone in middle school), I found myself out of the circle of friends I'd once had and aimlessly looking for direction. Luckily, my mom stepped in. As with any activity, I had to start at the beginning. The part of Flying Monkey #2, although not the largest part in *The Wizard of Oz*, was still emotionally and psychologically fulfilling. I conquered my fear of public speaking and made new friends. The years that followed seem somewhat of a blur to me now. I had the right combination of talent and dedication for the groups that I was a part of, and I became completely engrossed in them. OPUS (school choir) and theater took over my life and kept motivating me through high school. Although I didn't like doing homework for AP calculus, I knew I had to do it in order to participate in the other activities. As my mom points out in her explanation, I started to apply myself to academic subjects the same way I did for music or film. My grades came up, I got into a great college, and in the end, I turned out just fine.

As an adult, I've encountered periods of uncertainty much like those I experienced in high school. Sometimes, when a big change occurs (such as graduating from high school or moving to New York City), I'm not sure where to focus my efforts. I may flounder for a bit as I search for that thing that will inspire me to action, but eventually I find that one thing that I can really dive into. I find that I am motivated to excel when I'm interested in something and when I feel that I have a chance to succeed. I have continued to be involved with the arts—sound design and a cappella groups—which I probably would not have found unless I had been allowed to pursue my earlier interests. Sometimes, you have to give your children the opportunities to succeed, even when they're struggling in other areas.

CHAPTER 8

Don't You Want to Be an Astronaut?

Providing Career Guidance by Helping Your Children Recognize Their Interests and Abilities

Success is liking yourself, liking what you do,
and liking how you do it.

~Maya Angelou

My children's career interests changed frequently as they grew up. I especially remember Jen's shifting interests, starting with the time she wanted to be an astronaut.

"Mom," she asked one day, "what do you have to do to become an astronaut?" Ever alert to the possibility of a promising career for my children, I perked up. "Well," I answered hesitantly, not wanting to appear too eager, "you have to study lots of math and science and be really good at them. Then, I'm not sure, but we could find out." Nodding, Jen seemed to be thinking, "I'm good at math and science. I could be an astronaut." At least that's what my interpretation was, but in reality, she was probably wondering what we would be having for dinner that night.

I was excited by the hope that we might have an astronaut in the family. I set to work immediately researching ways to promote my daughter's burgeoning interest. I discovered Space Camp, and soon my nine-year-old daughter was packed up and sent to Florida for the week, where she learned how to plan a space mission and also consumed lots of freeze-dried ice cream.

When I picked her up at the airport, I eagerly inquired, "Well, what did you think?"

"It was cool," she replied, "Can we go home now?" But that was it. No more mention about wanting to be an astronaut. My daughter's brilliant career—or, more accurately, my brilliant vicarious career—appeared to have evaporated.

"Did something happen at Space Camp?" I asked.

"What do you mean?" Jen answered.

"I don't know—did someone pick on you? Was camp not fun?"

"No, it was lots of fun. I got to plan a mission," my daughter replied.

"What happened to wanting to be an astronaut?" I asked.

"Mom, I never said I wanted to be an astronaut," Jen said with startling clarity for a nine-year-old. "You just wanted me to."

After that, as I watched Jen's interests continue to shift and evolve, I never again mistook a passing interest for her final career choice, although my husband and I did make the mistake of setting up an entire darkroom when Jen mentioned that she might be interested in photography. In fact, one Christmas was dedicated entirely to gifts in this area—a camera, a kit for developing pictures, and a tripod. It was so extreme that Jen commented, "I do like other things, you know. Clothes would be nice."

Multipotentiality

One of the issues that perplex gifted children as they grapple with understanding their interests and abilities and think about future careers is *multipotentiality*. A person with multipotentiality is defined as "any individual who, when provided with appropriate environments, can select and develop any number of competencies to a high level."[54] A gifted child with multipotentiality may love to read and read at a very high level. She may also love math and be performing two grade levels ahead of her same-age peers in that subject. In addition, she may keep a journal and enjoy science and be able to plan advanced investigations. In short, gifted children with multipotentiality seem to have a keen interest and above-average ability in many areas.

For these children, the sky is the limit, and so well-meaning adults often say to them, "You can be anything you want to be!" Indeed, we live in a free country, so it seems that with enough effort, anyone should be able to be whatever he or she wants to be. Right? The problem is that when we say this to children who exhibit multipotentiality, we do not provide the type of guidance that enables them to develop an awareness of the factors that go into choosing a career—strengths, interests, values, and goals—an awareness that, if developed, will empower them to select appropriate careers that will satisfy them and make them happy. If they do not develop this awareness, two problems occur. First, they may not make a fully informed decision and may select a career in which they are not happy. Second—and this could be the more difficult problem—they may get caught up in multiple interests, pursuing one after another but never sticking with anything long enough to achieve a high level of proficiency or accomplishment

Picture this: Mark is a college student with many interests and abilities. He read at a college level while in middle school. He is good at writing and also in math. Because of his advanced reading skills, he has developed an interest in nonfiction books. Last year, he read biographies of early 20th century Supreme Court justices, and so he thought he might want to enter law after graduation. He took classes so that he could become pre-law. However, early last semester, he decided that math was also appealing, and so he took classes in advanced theoretical math and switched his major. Now he's not so sure, wondering if he should be investigating a journalism career as well. He's just not ready to commit!

You can see how, if this pattern continues, it could become a problem. It's not that we don't want our children to have fun exploring different interests and options, but eventually they must commit to something. It takes years and years to focus and become proficient in a career, and if we never commit, we may never acquire the proficiency required to advance in our chosen career. Adults must therefore learn how to guide gifted children toward discovering where their values, activities, skills, and interests lie—and do so in an age-appropriate manner.

It should be noted that the concept of multipotentiality in the field of gifted education is a debated one. Some researchers are beginning to rethink the topic, suggesting that multipotentiality may be an artifact of tests that do not adequately measure the advanced abilities of gifted students.[55] They suggest that if these children were appropriately tested with assessments using higher ceilings, a different profile of interests and abilities would emerge.

Guiding Gifted Children

As parents, we can help our children explore the components (values, activities, skills, and interests) that relate to happy and successful careers. Along the way, we may learn that our children are interested in many things, and these interests may or may not turn into career possibilities. We want to offer reasonable guidance, not forcing them into one career, yet providing them with a variety of exploratory experiences. However, there's a catch. If we don't provide enough guidance, a talented child may drift from one area to another and never focus on one interest, experiencing a type of paralysis when it's time to choose a single career path.

A similar pattern can be seen with some gifted children if you look at their curricular and extracurricular involvements. For example, a gifted high school junior might be a cheerleader, captain of the girls' soccer team, president of Honor Society, a member of Key Club, play clarinet in the school band, and a volunteer at a local homeless shelter, while also taking several Advanced Placement courses. She is talented in many areas but spread so thin that she has little time for sleep or relaxation. It's helpful for this child to realize that she can't do everything and that she would benefit from learning to set priorities. She can list the pros and cons of each activity and select which ones to keep and which ones to give up.

What are appropriate experiences that parents can use to guide their children toward rewarding future careers? Before we discuss these, it is important to recognize two facts: (1) our children may eventually start out in one career but will probably work in several careers during their lifetime, and (2) the most rewarding careers are ones that bring happiness and satisfaction, and they are the result of considering not only interests and strengths, but also values and goals. Letting your child know that the first career he chooses may not necessarily be his final career choice may take the pressure off of him at key decision points, such as when applying to college. Additionally, a gifted child may be interested in and good at many things, but considering what his goals are and what he values may guide him toward making a better decision.

The career guidance process may start as early as elementary school, when you help your child begin exploring her interests.[56] Researchers[57] suggest that as a parent, you need to assist your child in finding her own identity. First, help her explore what's out there by exposing her to extracurricular activities such as math and science clubs, writing competitions, drama, and more. Also consider informal experiences such as hobbies. Would she like to collect rocks? How about taking up calligraphy? You might participate in a "Bring Your Child to Work" day, which is great way to allow your child to see how your day unfolds. Listen to your child as she describes her interests, but don't fixate on one specific career, for young children often do not understand enough about themselves (or the jobs) to make these types of decisions.

During middle school, you can begin to help your child uncover his strengths and interests, as well as his values and goals. Suggest that he make a list of interests and things that he likes to do. Are there any careers that would allow him to continue to expand his experience with these interests? Are there careers that combine two or more of the interests?

This may be a time for more structured types of experiences, such as job shadowing or interviewing someone in a particular career. Sometimes such an experience results in the child saying, "Oh, it's not like I thought it was; I'm not interested in that anymore." For example, many children like animals and think they would like to be a veterinarian. When they job shadow for a few hours in a vet's office, though, they may reconsider, saying, "I think the pain, blood, and heavy responsibilities are more than I anticipated."

If the child still likes the career, it may be time to locate a mentor. Encourage your child to imagine herself in the role of the professional. What are the tasks of some of the different careers that interest her? What sort of education does each career require? What would a typical day be like? When would she report to work? How would she manage the stresses of the job? Does she like what she sees in her mind's eye? Guide the conversation toward values and goals, considering a variety of questions. Does she want to help others? Does she want to earn a large salary? Does she want to work with people, or does she envision herself working primarily with objects such as computers or laboratory equipment? These types of questions target lifestyle concerns, which are every bit as important as interests and strengths.

To be able to guide your child appropriately, you must be knowledgeable about the types of careers that are now and will be available in the future. One resource that you might consider using and sharing with your child is the U.S. Bureau of Labor's *Occupational Outlook Handbook*, which provides information on hundreds of jobs. On the Bureau of Labor's website (see the appendix of this book), you can search for individual occupations and explore the nature of the work, educational requirements, expected job prospects, working conditions, current earnings, and more.

During high school, a child may extend his formal experiences to include volunteer opportunities and paid positions. Why not let him try out his leadership in a role as a camp counselor? Can he work at a hospital? Of course, he may continue to be involved with extracurricular activities at an even deeper level, serving in leadership positions in after- or before-school clubs.

Unfortunately, high school can be a trying time for both parents and children, especially during the senior year when decisions about college are usually made. Many parents and children make the mistake of thinking that the college they select locks the child into a future career, which is not at all the case. If the child is not sure about what career she wishes to eventually select, she can choose a college that offers a variety of majors. It is also time to remind her that her initial career need not be her final career.

Career guidance should be a continual process from the elementary years onward—a process that ultimately guides children into rewarding careers of the child's choosing. Remember that these decisions need to be based on years of careful consideration that take into account the child's strength, abilities, interests, values and goals, always keeping in mind the awareness that nothing is written in stone, and nothing is final. The most important things to do are to establish a dialogue and to respect, as always, the individuality that resides within your child.

Table 8.1. Parenting Strategies to Provide Career Guidance to Gifted Children

✔ Avoid steering your child toward one career.

✔ Expose your child to a variety of clubs and extracurricular opportunities that may help her explore her strengths and interests.

✔ Actively discuss your child's strengths and interests with her.

✔ Help your child think about her values. What does she value when envisioning a career? Working with people? Making the world a better place? Working to stimulate her intellectual curiosity? Assess these periodically over time as she matures.

✔ Help your child think about her goals. What does she want to do in a career? Make more money? Have more time? Be flexible in her working hours? Gain prestige? Assess these periodically over time as she matures.

✔ As your child matures, help her consider the compromises involved with specific careers. For example, if she becomes a doctor, she may make more money, but she may have less flexibility in her personal time.

Afterword by Jen

Mom is being too hard on herself. There actually was a time when I did want to be an astronaut. She seems to be forgetting my space-themed bat mitzvah, complete with a life-sized Captain Picard cut-out. So these professional ambitions she had for me weren't entirely the results of wishful thinking. There was often genuine interest on my part, and Mom and Dad paid me the compliment of taking me seriously, even as I changed plans from year to year (or from week to week). I'm grateful that they erred on the side of taking me too seriously rather than, like those horrible parents in Roald Dahl's *Matilda*, mocking my interests or simply ignoring them.

I'm writing the afterword to this chapter because I picked a career that my parents didn't foresee for me—one that even disturbed them a little bit, at least at first. When I reached my sophomore year of college, I found myself living the cliché of the English/philosophy/art history major who loves what she does but can't bring her parents to understand it. In my case, it was religious studies. I took a class in Jewish history with a wonderful professor, and I was hooked. "What will you do with a degree in that?" my parents asked. "What about something more practical, like economics? Or biology?"

I think it was more than worries about its practicality, though. Religion is a loaded subject. Everyone has an opinion, and it's not as simple as where you should go for dinner one night. It's on where you're going for eternity. Studying religion in an academic context isn't about judging anyone's morals or pronouncing on the existence of God, but I find that when I tell people what I do, I often get the reaction that ministers and police officers hate. People straighten up, stop cursing, and reconsider the drinks in their hands. Then they tell me about their favorite Bible passages or explain why they haven't been to synagogue recently. These are people old enough to be my parents or grandparents, people who lead productive and meaningful lives. These are not people whom I have any place judging, and yet they seem to feel that I do. Maybe I need to work on my delivery.

Given that dynamic, it was probably inevitable that my parents would feel some discomfort about my career choice. Maybe they thought I would judge their choices. Maybe they worried that I would bring the constant national conflict over the place of religion in public life into their home. Maybe I'm projecting and they didn't worry about any of this at all. I do know that I felt anxiety from them that went beyond concern over whether I would be able to support myself, and I'm constructing possible reasons for it from the few conversations we had on the topic. I was uncomfortable, too. I knew something about my choice bothered them. I take their opinions seriously, and I wondered, since they were really worried about my ability to support myself, whether I should worry about the same thing. It occurred to me that religion, like English or philosophy, might not be a serious enough topic of study to merit the time and money all three of us were investing in my education.

It's a little strange to be writing a book like this and not include a deeper discussion about this conflict, but the truth is, it wasn't really necessary. The discomfort I'm describing, on both our parts, was relatively short-lived. I looked into career possibilities and found that our worries were overblown. I would never be insanely wealthy, but I had a good chance at fulfilling work that could support a family. As I allayed my own doubts, I was able to do the same for my parents, and they grew less concerned.

More than that, though, they saw that my interest in religion only deepened with time. We also found some common ground in the subject. I moved toward an emphasis on religious history, and history has always been a shared hobby for my family. (Did I say hobby? I meant obsession. How many American children can describe all of Henry VIII's wives and the religious conflicts he ignited?) I talked to them about my work, and I think they began to see how similar it was to the topics they had taught me to love in my childhood. They began asking me questions about dealing with historical sources, about possible economic and political causes for religious movements, and about the personalities I loved so much in the materials I was studying. They made the effort to talk about aspects of my work that they could appreciate—ones they might have enjoyed studying themselves. We do still fight about the place of religion in public life, but those debates are not the first, the last, or even the most spirited of the political arguments that occasionally overtake our family gatherings. We argue over dinner, we make the same points we've always made, and when we get tired of it, we have some dessert and let it go.

Mom claims that I imagined a lot more initial opposition from them than I really faced, and she's probably right. But that is part of our parent-child dynamic. I expected displeasure and exaggerated the little they did express because I wanted to please them. On the other hand, their hesitation pushed me to think harder about my choice, its possible disadvantages, and the reasons I picked it. Their love of history and their constant encouragement of my interests through childhood made that a lot easier.

Navigating this challenge was much more about coming to an understanding of myself, independent from my parents, than the other chapters on which I've commented. This was about learning to look at my parents, with their loving and well-intentioned beliefs about who I would become, and tell them that they weren't quite right. I suppose if you take anything from this chapter, it should be that you can guide your child and help him to explore many interests. You can, and should, help him to identify his strengths. In the end, though, it's up to him to bring it all together. It was because my parents guided me to know myself and trust my instincts about what would make me happy that I was able to find the right career. Even though it wasn't what they would have envisioned for me, they took it pretty well; I just had to trust them—and myself—enough to do it.

CHAPTER 9

If It's Too Hard, Then Quit!

Encouraging Persistence in Your Gifted Child

Diamonds are only lumps of coal that stuck to their jobs.
~B. C. Forbes

Sarah's fourth-grade teacher conducted a classroom spelling bee, and the top two or three children in that competition went on to compete in the school-wide spelling bee. At first, Sarah didn't pay a lot of attention to the spelling bee, probably because the words were easy and she felt confident about the next level. On the day of the school's spelling bee, she didn't appear overly anxious, bounding out the door in her usual "I'm going to take on the world" way. And she did. Easily spelling word after word, she sailed through the competition, earning herself a place in the district's spelling bee. It was at this point that things got serious.

One day, several weeks before the district competition, Sarah appeared with a book I'd never seen before. "What's that?" I asked.

"My word list," she replied. "We're studying it."

"Who's studying it?" I inquired.

"Everyone from the school who's going to be in the district's spelling bee," she answered. "We're all studying with the principal.

He calls us down to his office, and he calls out the words. We spell them. It helps us practice."

I picked up the book and scanned the list. *Abscissa. Macrocephalous. Hyssop.* Wow, these were difficult words. "I can see why you're studying them," I replied. Nodding seriously, my 10-year-old daughter grabbed the book from my hands, scampered off, and closed the door to her room.

Over the next few weeks, Sarah prepared for the bee, but not excessively. She studied for a half hour here or 15 minutes there, but not on a regular basis. "How are your words coming?" I would ask. "Okay," she nodded, and that would be that. As the date of the spelling bee grew closer, however, I noticed some doubts creeping in.

"Mom, what if I fail? What if I bomb on the first or second word? "

"Well, what if you do?" I replied. "It won't be the end of the world. Besides, you're studying, right?" Slowly, she nodded her head, and I looked for a way to change the subject. I wondered, *Did my daughter want to quit? Should I let her quit to avoid a potentially painful experience?*

The day of the bee came, and Sarah screwed up her courage for the event. Her head was raised, and there was a fierce gleam in her eyes. I was proud of her. We trooped *en masse* with the entire family to the regional spelling bee, wished Sarah luck, kissed her forehead for additional luck, and sent her off to sit with the other contestants at the front of the room. We took our places in the parents' section with 25 other nervous families.

The first round came and went. Sarah drew an easy word and spelled it with ease. Many other students drew similarly easy words; few were eliminated during that first round. A warm-up round, I thought. The next round, however, proved to be more difficult, and several contestants were eliminated. I glanced at my daughter and saw the look of concentration on her face. Was that good? Or was she still anxious?

When it was Sarah's turn again, she stepped up to the microphone. There came the pause that preceded each contestant's word, and our family sat on the edges of our chairs. "*Herbaceous,*" boomed the voice of the caller.

My daughter stepped closer to the microphone. "Herbaceous," she repeated slowly. "May I have a definition, please?"

"Herbaceous," came the reply. "Adjective. Pertaining to an herb."

Another pause. "Herbaceous," began Sarah. "H…e…r…b…a…c…." Pause. We held our breath. She continued, "i…" Before we knew what had happened in our state of focused attention, we heard a bell ring. Oh, no! That was the bell that meant, "Incorrect!" It meant, "You're done. Remove yourself from the stage." It meant, "You failed."

I can still remember the moment, even though it's now 15 years later. I remember Sarah's stunned expression and how I thought she looked paralyzed. "She won't be able to walk off stage," I fretted. "Then what? Will I have to go up and carry her off? How embarrassing would that be for her?" Just as I was rising from my seat to lead her off stage, she suddenly sprang to life. Sprinting, she ran down the steps of the stage, tears pouring down her face. Blindly, she ran past where we were all sitting, down the aisle, and out through the room's big double doors.

I found her trembling outside of the room. I ran up to her and placed my arms around her, pulling her to me. I could feel the tears falling on my shoulder. "Why are you so upset?" I asked, genuinely puzzled by my daughter's fierce reaction. She managed to speak between the sobs, "I failed. I got out on the second word. I'm so stupid!" I hugged her to me tighter, unsure of what to say or how to comfort her. At that moment, the superintendent for our school district happened to walk by. Noticing Sarah, she paused and then joined us, pulling Sarah gently down to sit with her on a nearby bench.

"What's your name?" she asked gently.

"Sa-Sa-Sarah," my daughter could barely get out between sobs.

"Sarah, why are you crying so hard?"

"Because I failed," came the answer. "I studied and studied and worked so hard, and I failed. It means I'm stupid. I'm no good

at spelling. I failed. I never want to enter a spelling bee again!"
Exhausted from the long explanation, Sarah burst into a fresh spate
of sobbing.

I'll never forget the superintendent's reaction or what came
next. She gently placed her arm around Sarah and pulled her close.
"Let me tell you something. You are not a failure. The very fact that
you're here is evidence of that. How many students are even invited
to the district bee? You are a champion, and champions sometimes
fail. This was your time."

Sarah paused in her sobs to consider this. Gradually, she
calmed down and the sobs stopped. She peered up into the superintendent's face. "Okay," she smiled, and her shoulders relaxed. The
crisis, at least for now, was over. I was grateful for the superintendent's words of wisdom. I knew that there would be other crises
ahead, though, and I feared that the process of helping Sarah deal
with her ups and downs would be a long one.

The Problem with Quitting

Gifted children sometimes lack the motivation to persist in
a task. Think of it: If you're good at school and every assignment
comes easily to you, if you never struggle to achieve good grades,
why would you try very hard? And if you've never had to try very
hard to achieve anything, the first time that you do have to try, it
can hit you like a ton of bricks. The first time that you struggle with
a difficult or more complex task may be the first time you realize
that you're not the best at something. And if your idea of who you
are is totally tied up in being the best, this realization may have
far-reaching consequences. For example, you may suddenly begin
to shy away from trying difficult things because you might fail, and
if you fail, your confidence and sense of self-esteem may fail along
with you. All of a sudden, you're not the quickest, brightest, sharpest
kid on the street, and so who are you? It's safer to stick with easier
tasks that don't require additional effort so that you can shine. This
complex line of reasoning may be why many gifted children are

averse to attempting challenging activities or why they shut down when they first encounter a difficult task.

For Sarah, a perfectionist, the spelling bee was an example of this. Sarah was always driving herself to achieve, sometimes at the price of her own happiness. Usually, she achieved whatever she set her sights on, and over time, her tendency to doubt herself and her abilities has softened. But doubt has gotten the better of her on more than one occasion.

Gifted children like Sarah can benefit greatly from discussions on the importance of persistence and how to deal with failure. I have a friend who understands these concepts because she teaches origami to children—and this isn't just any type of origami; it's origami with attitude. Instead of folding delicate swans and paper cranes, Rachel has the children fold intricate, three-dimensional polyhedrons such as octagons, nonagons, and dodecahedrons. During the process, the children learn about folding, mathematics, and so much more.

Rachel tells a story about how she often enters a classroom with a very advanced origami shape such as a dodecahedron, and the children all ooh and ahh over the shape. One child will inevitably ask, "Can I have that?" Smiling, Rachel will reply, "No, but I will teach you how to make it." She starts by having the children fold a simple cube, but she then quickly allows the children to advance to more difficult shapes. At some point along the way, a child in the group will want to give up. "I can't do this," the child will cry. "I want to quit! It's too hard." Rachel will walk over to the child, put her arm around his shoulder, and say to him, "Stay in the struggle."

Stay in the struggle. What a simple idea, and yet an idea with so many consequences! If we don't "stay in the struggle," we don't accomplish much. We drop out of projects, we drop out of classes, and we may even drop out of life. We don't live up to commitments, and we let others down. Our reputation is shot, and we find ourselves, middle-aged or elderly, never having accomplished or built very much in our lives, all because we never learned how to "stay in the struggle."

It all starts very innocently when we are children. Parents, understandably, want to protect their young ones and so often avoid situations in which their children experience any discomfort, pain, or failure, and yet it is from these negative situations that we often grow. Children who are never allowed to suffer a failure never learn how to recover from it. Children who are always allowed to quit when a task becomes too hard grow up believing that the proper way to handle a difficult situation is to withdraw, a belief that can lead to an unfulfilled life. What Sarah endured in the spelling bee I believe paid off in the end. It was not to be her final bee, and although she never progressed past the regional level, she did not break down again. I noted in her as she matured a growing resilience and an ability to weather difficult tasks, as well as criticism. She fretted and worried less, learning each time that her world did not collapse if she did not perform perfectly. She persisted.

The Nature of Persistence

It's important to discuss with your children the nature of persistence. Frequently, children do not understand that difficult things can sometimes be extremely rewarding. They live in the moment, and if they are happy, they are happy. If they are sad, they may have difficulty imagining that the situation will improve. You can help by pointing out that at times, everyone experiences difficulties, but with persistence and effort, things usually get better. Select someone whom your child admires, and chat with your child about this individual. For instance, as a sophomore basketball star, Michael Jordan tried out for his high school varsity team, but he didn't make it because the coach believed he didn't have what it takes. However, after a year on the junior varsity squad, Jordan returned and tried out again, and due to his persistence and effort, he made the team. Of course, he went on to become one of the most outstanding athletes of all time.

Another example of courage and persistence, this time in a woman, can be found in the story of Joan of Arc. Most children are familiar with (and fascinated by) the legend. Born as a peasant girl in France in the early part of the 15th century, Joan was convinced that she had holy visions that she would lead her country to a great victory in the war against England. Most derided her. After all, in the middle ages, women weren't exactly considered fit for battle! After many setbacks, Joan was able to gain an audience with King Charles VII, who was impressed by her persistence and sincerity. Joan went on to lead her country to several great victories before her martyrdom at the age of 19 in 1431. In her story, which echoes down through the ages, we are impressed by her courage, persistence, and the strength of her convictions.

Other examples abound. Temple Grandin persisted through the realization that she was autistic, going on to develop major work in the field of animal husbandry. Jane Goodall spent decades working in the field and founded the Jane Goodall Institute, devoted to the preservation and research of primates in the wild. Sojourner Truth broke free of slavery and became a lecturer for the emancipation of women 50 years before women got the vote. Nelson Mandela persisted through 27 years of prison for his efforts against apartheid and went on to win the Nobel Peace Prize in 1993. In an age of fast everything (fast cars, fast food, and get-rich-quick thinking come to mind), our children are richer for hearing stories of persistence and planning for the long term.

Obviously, it is inappropriate to blindly force your child to continue with a task, for some activities or situations may truly be harmful to children. For example, consider a child who is bullied by the members of his baseball team. This situation has to be remedied, or if it is beyond remedying, it may be appropriate to allow the child to withdraw. How can you know when it's okay to let your child withdraw from an activity in which he no longer wishes to participate? Common sense plays a role, especially if you know your child well. However, it's also important to examine the activity.

Begin by examining the nature of the activity. If the activity is required and is one which your child is capable of accomplishing, it's important that you encourage him to stick it out. Josh came to me once asking to withdraw from the gifted program. However, his father and I had evidence from the assessment performed by the school district that indicated that he was capable of succeeding in the program, and so my answer was a firm, "No way."

Next, consider *who* is initiating the need to drop out. It may be the child, or it may be you, the parent. Either way, motives need to be considered. Why does the child wish to drop out? Is it a social need? A fear? A desire to do another activity? Why do you want the child to drop out? Perhaps you dread the time required by the activity or you fear failure on the part of your child.

It is important to consider the child's best interests in order to understand what the real problem is and what a viable solution (other than dropping out) might be. In the case of the bullied child on the baseball team, a first step might be for the parent to speak with the coach and inform him that the situation is occurring. If this puts an end to the bullying, great! If not, other steps may need to be taken, and if the situation can't be resolved, the child may have to drop out, hopefully switching to another team. Even then, an important lesson is communicated to the child: Quitting is the last resort. Solutions abound; don't give up easily.

Dealing with Boredom

At the other extreme, children frequently tire of activities and wish to withdraw from them simply because they are bored. Gifted children may become bored more easily than other children, and sometimes parents and teachers judge these children harshly, mistaking boredom for laziness or defiance. Often, the lessons or activities that the gifted child completes in the classroom are designed to teach content she already knows.[58] The problem is exacerbated in that gifted children often require fewer repetitions to learn something, or they've already learned it and are ready for new challenges. For example, if your daughter is a gifted artist and she's enrolled in a basic art class, she may not be working at a level that challenges her. Talk with her teacher to see if she's correctly placed.

However, it's also important that parents communicate the message that if a commitment has been made, it's vital to see it through. You can't force your child to continue to dance forever, but you can pick a milestone that finishes up a commitment. For example, a parent might say, "You don't want to dance anymore? You can't quit until the end-of-the year recital. You've made a commitment to the troupe." Or, " You want to drop out of the play? What about the other actors? Nope. You're in it until the play is over." Of course, it's best if you've established this rule ahead of time. When your daughter is begging to take dance lessons and you're at the store, outfitting her with leotards, dance shoes, and tights, it's prudent to say, "You realize that you're in this for the long haul, until the recital is over. No quitting!" This strategy sets up the expectation that she will at least see it through until then—that quitting is not an option.

At the same time you're communicating the message that quitting is inappropriate, it's important to support your child's struggle. This means that you do whatever is necessary to help your child through difficulties. Talking with him so that he can communicate his hopes and fears about the activity is an important beginning. Try to talk with him about how he's doing in the activity or with the task. Find out what the stumbling blocks are, and help him brainstorm ways to overcome them. And always let him know that you're there for him and that you support him.

Task Mastery and Task Performance

You can also talk with your child about the importance of task mastery versus task performance. Recall from Chapter 1 that there are two types of learners: those who place importance on mastering a task for the sake of learning to do the task, and those who place importance on mastering the task because they wish to avoid negative consequences or because they wish to look good in the eyes of others.[59] The first type of approach is often called *task mastery*, the second is called *task performance*, and these terms have nothing to do with liking or loving the task. Instead, they have to do with how one approaches learning. If you approach a task believing that it's important to master it for the sake of acquiring the skills or knowledge, you are exhibiting a task mastery approach. If, instead, you try the task because you want to look good to others or because you're afraid of being punished for not doing it, you're exhibiting a task performance approach. Over and over again, task mastery has been associated with numerous positive benefits, including increased academic achievement, motivation, and persistence. Helping your child develop a task mastery approach may therefore better equip her to learn more while she engages in an activity, to be more motivated, and to persist in her efforts.

How can you begin to develop a task mastery approach in your child? You need to start by talking with your child about the positive aspects of the activity. What is fun about it? What is important? What is engaging or interesting? Emphasize that the task or activity itself has merit and that it's not about how well he does it as compared with others. If he's not the best skier in the world, oh well. Also, emphasize that the important thing is to measure his own growth over time. Maybe he's not the best skier, but perhaps he's improved tremendously since his first visit to the slopes. Point out this progress: "Look at you! You couldn't even stand up on the skis when we first came here, but you just made your first successful downhill run!" Encourage him to internalize his own progress rather than compare himself to others.

We can't always prevent our children from quitting, but our goal should be to minimize their desire to do so. By allowing our children to struggle, we encourage endurance. By allowing them to fail sometimes, we encourage success. By supporting and loving them as they endure struggles, we send the message that we're there for them.

Sarah finished the spelling bee and went on to take part in others. I'd like to think this was due at least in part to her father and me encouraging her to persist in this difficult task, as well as the superintendent's encouraging words. Children need encouragement, and they need parents who know when to say, "You need to stick with this and see it through." I'm sure Sarah learned from these experiences, and today she has earned the "gift" of persistence, a not-inconsequential trait that serves her well.

Table 9.1. Parenting Strategies to Develop Persistence in Gifted Children

✔ Discuss the importance of persistence with your child. Provide examples of admired individuals who persisted through difficulties.

✔ Set and agree upon a milestone—an event that must take place before your child may withdraw from an activity.

✔ Support your child through struggles. Discuss the task or activity with him. Brainstorm solutions to problems that may arise. Let your child know that you're there to help him.

✔ Encourage a task mastery approach in your child. Remind him to measure his own progress and not to compare himself to others.

✔ Exhaust all solutions before allowing your child to withdraw from an activity, and only do so if it is vital to his physical or psychological health. Talk with your child about how quitting is a "last resort."

✔ If your child must withdraw from an activity, encourage him to replace it with a healthier alternative.

Afterword by Sarah

Persistence is an eerily appropriate topic in my life right now. I am trying to finish a Ph.D. in neurobiology, but I am not close enough to the end that I can celebrate or take the degree for granted. At particularly low points, I know to call my parents because they understand that I desperately want to finish, no matter what the latest setback has made me say. I don't remember a time when my parents struggled to get me to complete my homework as a child, but suddenly that's what I need! My mother has advised me to set aside a certain amount of time each day to do the part of my work that I loathe. Sooner than I know it, she promises, it will be finished. I'm getting more done under her plan, and so I'm less likely to quit.

I can definitely say that my parents successfully instilled in me persistence in the face of adversity. From my perspective, what is more difficult is determining when it is appropriate to quit and when I should persist. The story of the spelling bee illustrates a time when I needed encouragement, but at other times, I needed guidance on when to stop. For example, when I was in high school, I played oboe in our band. Maybe you're under the impression that the oboe creates beautiful music, but I can assure you that when played poorly, an oboe sounds quite similar to a dying duck. I was not particularly talented, didn't enjoy playing the oboe, and was not socially connected to most of the other band members. Nevertheless, I stuck with it, despite my parents' messages to me after the first year that it would be acceptable to stop. I stuck it out for several years. Indeed, I like to say that it was the worst mistake I ever made not once, but four times! I was convinced that it would pay off somehow, although in retrospect, I don't think that it did. One lesson I did walk away with, however, is that I need to examine more closely my reasons for sticking with an activity, even when I don't seem to be getting any benefit from it.

Children don't always have the ability to figure out when to quit and when to persist; I think only experience teaches you that. Parents, with the wisdom of years and perhaps a more reasonable perspective, are in a position to guide their children's choices. There will be times when children need to persist and times when they shouldn't. You, as the parent, should at all times be willing and able to help them evaluate the pros and cons of each path. I was stubborn and stayed in band despite the negatives, but honestly, I wish I'd listened to my mom and dad!

CHAPTER 10

Can't You Color Inside the Lines?

Nurturing Your Gifted Child's Creativity

Imagination is more important than knowledge.

~Albert Einstein

I was conducting a professional development workshop on creativity once when a teacher told a rather sad story. She related how, as a small child, she loved to draw and spent many happy hours with crayons and paper. Once, when she was in primary school, her teacher passed out supplies and told the class that each student should draw a picture of a horse. Dutifully, the child tried to comply, yet as she drew, the horse's shape became less and less definite. She drew gracefully and abstractly, revealing how the horse appeared to her mind's eye. When she was finished, she had drawn a picture of a shape that was as graceful and fleeting as the wind. Staring at the picture, she admired its curved lines, its smooth but crisp colors. It was perhaps the best picture she had ever completed, and she raised her hand to call her teacher over, eager to share its beauty.

"What's that?" asked the teacher as she looked over the drawing.

"It's my horse," said the child, gazing happily at the picture.

"I can't tell that it's a horse," said the teacher. "It helps if you stay in the lines."

Together, they both stared at the picture, only this time the child looked at it with the teacher's eyes. As the teacher withdrew, the little girl silently crumpled the work that had been so precious to her and slipped the ball of paper into her desk.

The adult teacher who related that story to me at the workshop was now in her forties. She said that she didn't voluntarily pick up a crayon or a paintbrush for the next 30 years, and she had only recently begun again to explore her passion for art. Thirty years of a gift…lost. Thirty years of a passion…wasted.

I've heard similar stories over and over, and I have to think that things have not improved much. Indeed, children who are especially creative appear to be at a distinct disadvantage in many of today's schools. Standardized testing preparation dictates curriculum and virtually every other classroom practice in our public schools, leaving precious little time for developing our children's creativity. Even in classes where creativity is supposedly at the heart of the subject, it is frequently stifled.

I worry sometimes that we are raising a generation who will know little beyond how to bubble in neat circles on score sheets using number 2 pencils. This is a shame, especially given the changing state of the global economy. Experts[60] warn that the current economic trend of shipping rote jobs overseas is likely to continue. Jobs that remain in the U.S. will be those that cannot be performed by rote—jobs that require creativity. We may therefore be heading toward a world in which future generations will be inadequately prepared to take their places, for memorization of rote facts or procedures will not enable them be gainfully employed. Rather, jobs in the future will probably require critical thinking, problem-solving skills, and creativity—all skills that are rarely taught in today's classrooms.

If you know that, with the current emphasis on standardized testing, your child's school allows teachers little time in the classroom to develop students' creativity, how can you as a parent recognize and nurture your child's creativity at home? How do we identify creative talent, and how do we develop it? To illustrate, I turn once again to my son Josh.

As I've already mentioned, Josh was the person in our family whom we identified as being creative. Whereas the girls were academically oriented and focused on achieving good grades, their brother was more laid back. Grades were not what motivated him, but as you'll recall, he *could* be motivated, and he *did* have talents. I noticed when Josh was very young that he had an outstanding visual memory. One day when he was four years old, we were watching a movie together when Josh turned to me and said, "Mom, that actor is the same man who was in…," and Josh named another movie we had seen a year before! That can't be, I thought. My very young son can't possibly recognize an actor from a movie that we saw a year before. And yet, peering at the actor, I recognized him, too—not at first, because the role he played was very different. But Josh was definitely right—it was the same actor. I wondered what it would mean that my son had this amazing visual acuity. Later, when Josh was older, I watched as his artistic skills developed. I still have the pencil sketch of the Donkey character from *Shrek* that he made for me in middle school.

I became interested in creativity because Josh was creative. You may have a child who is creative, and yet you may not—as I did not—recognize it as a talent. Children who are creative need to have that creativity validated, and recognizing their talent is the first step toward that validation. So with that in mind, let's explore creativity.

Understanding Creativity

Creativity is a misunderstood concept in our society. For example, we could play a game in which I ask you to think of three creative people, and you would probably think of famous creative people whom you have learned about through the years. Names such as Picasso, Dali, and Mozart might spring to mind. Notice that all of these individuals are associated with the arts—painting and music. Relatively few people would name individuals such as Bill Gates, founder of Microsoft, or Sonya Sotomayor, Supreme Court Justice, as being creative. Yet try to imagine the insight and creativity that these individuals must possess to have reached their position in life. You don't start a multi-billion-dollar company without having many good ideas, and you don't rise to the highest court in the land without having outstanding problem-solving skills. It becomes evident, then, that we are confused as to what exactly creativity is and how we define it. Does creativity include the ability to come up with many good ideas, no matter whether the ideas are associated with industry or the arts? Does it include problem-solving skills that we all use to some degree? What, exactly, is creativity?

Scholars have been trying to define creativity for years, and their views of creativity and creative individuals have evolved over time. In the 19th century, creative individuals were often viewed with suspicion, as some scholars believed that creative individuals possessed dysfunctional brains! A hundred years ago, our view of who was creative consisted mostly of artists, musicians, painters, dancers, and writers, and this notion of creativity informed public school curriculum throughout much of the 20th century. Slowly, however, our views of creativity have begun to change. More recently, scholars and others have helped shape our growing understanding of creativity. Two concepts are particularly important for parents to understand.

First, creativity is about more than the arts. It is also about coming up with many ideas, evaluating those ideas, and problem solving. Everyone needs and uses these skills in life, and so everyone possesses at least some degree of creativity. By the way, the type of creativity that we use in everyday life is "creativity" with a lower-case "c," as opposed to "Creativity" with a capital "C," which is more obvious and universally recognized as outstanding talent. Wolfgang Mozart, Albert Einstein, Salvador Dali, and Bill Gates all demonstrate big-C Creativity because they were able to offer creative products that changed their fields in a dramatic way. On the other hand, most of the rest of us demonstrate little-c creativity, or creativity that we use every day to solve problems and generate ideas in our lives.

The second significant concept is that lowercase-c creativity may be taught and encouraged. It should perhaps be included in school curriculum planning in order for students to take their places in jobs of the future that will, in all likelihood, require more of this type of creativity. As more outsourcing of routine jobs occurs, scholars[61] suggest that the ability to think creatively about problems and their solutions will be in more demand than ever.

What does all of this mean for your child? It means a number of things. It's possible that your child could be creative with a capital "C," and if this is the case, it's certainly important to identify and encourage that creativity. But if she's not (and let's face it, most of us are not Mozart), she can still be creative with a lowercase "c" in everyday life or in her future work, and it's important to develop this kind of creativity as well. Children who are big-C Creative are easy to spot—they're the ones who are composing sonatas at the age of eight, or painting masterpieces at age nine, or writing novels at age 10. I'm using these ages loosely to make the point that this type of Creativity jumps out at you—at everyone. There is usually no debate about whether it exists or not, whereas creativity with a lowercase "c" is more difficult to spot. You may see it in your child as a preference for writing—perhaps she keeps a journal or writes poetry. Or she may play with watercolors and other types of paints for hours on end. She may not be painting masterpieces, but she may enjoy experimenting with different media, and you may begin to see what you can identify as the beginnings of good work.

What do you do with a child who has artistic abilities, especially when some schools have few or no programs in the arts? First, it's important to allow your child to explore various mediums. If he loves to play with watercolors, allow him to experiment with charcoal or chalk. If he loves to play classical music, expose him to jazz. You also need to find a teacher or mentor in the child's area of talent. This person may be the most objective and qualified person to assess your child's true talent. As parents, we are not experts in all fields, and we may be biased. We want our children to be talented, and they may be, but sometimes we read more into their abilities than we should. Ask your child's teacher or mentor to assess his true abilities, but discuss the findings away from your child. You need to know what the teacher thinks of your child's abilities, but sometimes the truth may not be what you expected, and you need to act as a reasonable buffer for this information.

Meet with your child's teacher privately to receive a true assessment of her talent, evaluate the information, and then discuss it with your child in truthful yet kind terms. You may even want to get a second opinion from someone considered an expert in the area of the talent. Whatever the outcome, you'll gain a realistic understanding of your child's talent. If you are satisfied with the teacher and feel that your child is learning and progressing in her skills, your child may stay with him for a while, sometimes even years, but she may also eventually outgrow the teacher's abilities. It's important for the teacher to discuss this with the parent, and you need to identify the next steps together. Is there another teacher who might be able to take the child's abilities further? Is there a special school where the child might study?

Traditional schools tend to reinforce the child with academic abilities in traditional subjects; they may not pay much attention to the development of the creatively or artistically gifted. A whiz at math? Great! Sign him up for the math club. He's wonderful! Reads two grade levels above her class? Super! Give her extra praise and buy her more books! Paints like a Picasso? Hmm…he already takes art once a week (with the other children). What to do? Here are some crayons. He can color during free time.

It is worth noting that the child who exhibits artistic abilities may have special social-emotional needs. Many schools have little knowledge and even less time to dedicate to artistically talented students, which may leave these students searching for ways to develop and express their talents. As athletics and popularity become more important in the upper grades, peers may come to view artistic children with suspicion because they are different. The same sensitivities that make them good artists may make gifted children shy away from social situations or may make them overly sensitive to criticism, resulting in a difficult adolescence. Encourage your child to join extracurricular clubs and other groups with a focus on his artistic side. Art clubs, drama clubs, and musical groups abound, and it may be through these clubs that your child starts to feel less isolated. Resources in the appendix of this book can help you learn more about social-emotional development in artistically talented children.

What about the child who exhibits few or no artistic abilities? Can she still be creative? Absolutely! All children can be creative in some way, and as we discussed before, it's important to develop their creative abilities to prepare them for their future lives and jobs in a world that will be more and more dependent on individual creativity.

Research[62] has suggested that creativity is comprised of a set of four abilities: originality, fluency, elaboration, and flexibility. Originality is the ability that enables you to come up with new and original ideas, such as new inventions. Fluency is the ability to come up with many ideas. For example, if I asked you to think of as many words that mean "red" as you can, you might suggest the following: rose, rustic, burgundy, ruby, crimson, and more. The more words you name, the more fluent you are. Elaboration means adding lots of detail to things. For instance, if I ask you to draw a picture of a man, and you draw a simple stick man, you are not elaborating. If, however, you draw a man and add eyes, ears, nose, mouth, hair, fingers, toes, shirt, shorts, shoes, hat, and freckles, you are elaborating. Flexibility consists of the ability to take an idea and add to it or use it for something else. Dean Kamen, the noted inventor who holds more than 150 patents, modified the dialysis machine to make it portable. Now many patients are able to undergo dialysis without traveling to a hospital. Research[63] suggests that these aspects or elements of creativity may be nurtured in children. Some ways to do this follow.

Helping Your Child Develop Creative Skills

One of the best ways to develop creative skills in your child is to play creativity games with him. One example is the "What-If" game. To play the game, simply construct a "what-if" statement that requires the child to think about the extreme or the silly. For example, "What if you woke up one day and all of the colors were gone from the world? What if everything were in black and white?" You and your child can then develop a list of consequences that might include answers such as:

- ✔ Rainbows would be less interesting or would not exist.
- ✔ Summer and fall leaves would look the same.
- ✔ People might stop seeing racial differences.
- ✔ Paintings would be less vibrant.
- ✔ It might be hard to tell when a stove burner is hot.

Developing this list together encourages your child's fluency and originality skills. To develop flexibility, try playing another game called "Think of all the possible uses for…." For example, ask your child to think of all the uses for a carrot. Together, you might come up with a list that ranges from the obvious to the obscure. As with the rules in brainstorming, all ideas are acceptable. Judgment and evaluation can kill creativity—the very thing we're trying to encourage. Ideas for using a carrot might include:

- ✔ As a snowman's nose
- ✔ As a pen (add ink to the end)
- ✔ As a doll's missing leg
- ✔ As a pointer
- ✔ As a candle (add a wick to the end)
- ✔ As a magic wand

Another type of creativity is problem solving, or the ability to identify a problem and work through to its solution. Think of how many times and various situations in which we use this skill in life. What should we buy for dinner at the market? Which outfit should I wear today? Will he make a good spouse? Should I let her try out for soccer? Why isn't he doing his homework? Life is full of situations that demand thinking and problem-solving skills, not only in our personal lives, but also in our professional lives. How do we teach our children these creative and critical thinking skills?

Alex Osborne systemized the process, developing a five-step method called the Creative Problem Solving (CPS) method,[64] which is widely used in industry today. This method has migrated into education and is also used in classrooms throughout the country. The five steps (which have been modified slightly over time) are:

1. Fact finding – Explore information surrounding the problem.
2. Problem finding – Determine the nature of the real problem.
3. Idea finding – Generate ideas to solve the problem.
4. Solution finding – Evaluate the ideas to come up with one or more viable solutions.
5. Acceptance finding – Publicize and develop support for the solution(s).

CPS may be used with children in a variety of situations. Once your child learns the five- step process, she can apply those steps to whatever problem she faces. For example, if she can't decide to which college(s) she should apply, CPS could help her clarify her goals regarding college. To help her get started, you might ask, "What's the real problem? Is it that you don't want to attend a large college? A small college? A rural college? Are you focusing more on the social life or the academic life? Does the variety of majors make a difference?" These questions represent the fact-finding stage of CPS. You might go on to discover that the real problem is that your teen can't decide if she's interested in science or art (problem finding). Together, you can then research a list of schools that offer strong majors in each area (idea finding) and study the merits of each school on the list (solution finding) until she feels comfortable with a few schools (acceptance finding).

It is worth mentioning here that over time, many children lose faith in their ability to be creative. Students enter kindergarten excited and happy, eager to interact with the world through play.

Indeed, play is the primary way that children experience creativity, for it is through play that they paint, draw, act, sing, dance, and generally express what is in their imaginations. However, as they grow older and school becomes more focused on achievement and test scores, they experience fewer and fewer opportunities for play. Children are encouraged to sit still, raise their hands, and provide the one correct answer, which leaves little room to express any creativity. As a result, by the time these children grow into adults, most of them will tell you that they are no longer creative. They may say that they work hard and they are smart, but many will say that they struggle with being creative. Consequently, the more that you, as a parent, point out when your child is exhibiting creativity (whether it's little "c" or big "C"), the more likely he will begin to believe and trust in his creative abilities.

Creativity for All

Whether your child is creative (with a lowercase "c") or Creative (with a capital "C"), it is possible with a little time and effort to provide opportunities for talent development. When you factor in the understanding that jobs in the future will require original and flexible thinking, you begin to realize how important it is for all of our children to develop their creative abilities.

Table 10.1. Parenting Strategies to Identify and Develop Your Gifted Children's Creativity

✔ For children who exhibit creative abilities:
  o Realistically assess your child's creativity. Is it big "C" or little "c"?
  o If you cannot realistically assess your child's abilities, take her to an expert (e.g., an art or music or dance teacher) who can.
  o Find a teacher/mentor who will take your child's abilities to the next level.

o Be alert for the possibility that your child may outgrow the teacher's abilities. Be prepared to take her to another teacher who can help her reach an even higher level.

o Be aware of your child's special social-emotional needs, which may accompany her creative abilities.

o Involve your child in extracurricular groups that will help her find others who are interested in the same area(s) (e.g., drama club).

✔ For all children:

o Understand types of creative abilities that may be developed in your child (e.g., flexibility, fluency, originality, elaboration).

o Play creativity games with your child to develop those abilities.

o Develop problem-solving abilities in your child by practicing the Creative Problem Solving method with her.

o Point out when your child is creative, and encourage this type of behavior.

Afterword by Josh

Creativity is a loose term that encompasses so many types of abilities, personalities, and learning experiences. When my mom mentions my particular creative abilities and habits (i.e., connecting faces to movies or sketching), she is writing more about my thought processes, not about my genius, because after all, if I were a *Creative* genius, I surely would have already written that great American novel or conducted the New York Philharmonic by now. Instead, I turned out to be a normal child who simply thought about things in a creative and different way.

I've already told you about some of the issues that I had with underachievement and how I overcame them by finding activities with which I could engage. This section focuses more on how I grew up as a creative child. To this day, I'm not certain whether I sought out creative endeavors or I was just naturally more inclined to participate in those activities. Either way, by the time I was in middle school, my abilities and interests clearly set me apart as the creative one in the family. I enjoyed drawing, making music, and pursuing something that was uniquely mine. While I did not excel in school the same way that my older sisters did, I was always aware that I had a different skill set and a drive for creating something new.

What I've noticed about being creative is that I think about everyday life differently than the other members of my family. My mind approaches a new activity in a strange way in that, although I am a little intimidated about starting a project, once I take the first leap, I need to know everything about the subject. There is never enough information to quench this thirst I have when I first become interested in a subject, which ties back into selective achievement.

The best example of this is the story of how I wound up in film school. Similar to the story of how I wound up in drama, I was urged to find something to occupy my time in high school other than taking naps on the couch. After taking art classes and learning the basics of painting and design, I wanted to try something else. Our high school offered a television production course, and after stepping inside the classroom, I knew I was home. During high school, I loved the arts, whether it was music, acting, or design. Film and television production had the right combination of all of my interests rolled into one. A film has a music score, a director has to be able to communicate with actors, and a director of photography has to know composition. I fell in love with the idea of making movies.

I eventually went on to attend New York University for a film degree. While I was there, I crafted my skills and learned about the business, but I still wrestled with the logistical side of making movies. For every massively creative aspect of birthing a film, there are three more logistical nightmares lurking around the corner. I quickly learned that although I was a creative student in the visual and musical sense, I struggled through the organizational side of the filmmaking process. I often needed help getting shoots produced, and I quickly realized that there were other types of creativity. Some of my peers were clever problem solvers. Because I loved the process of making films and the end product, I focused my efforts and watched and learned every chance I could get, trying to understand the creative problem-solving process. Eventually I got the hang of it, and now I can handle that side of production.

Being creative doesn't always mean writing a sonata or painting the "Mona Lisa" but instead takes on the idea of thinking about a situation in a different way. There were many times during my childhood when my parents saw an issue arise in me similar to one that had already shown up in one of my sisters, but they had to switch gears in order to resolve that issue with me simply because I responded differently. While I struggled in school, my parents never threatened to take away the creative aspects in my life (filmmaking, music, theater) because they knew that those things provided an important creative outlet. They knew that I was motivated in those activities, and removing them would have had a negative effect on my other schoolwork.

It's important to not only notice creativity in children, but also to nurture it and allow your children to follow it to their dreams.

Afterword by the Author

What Does It All Mean?

An ounce of action is worth a ton of theory.
~Ralph Waldo Emerson

At the start of our journey together, I compared parenting to canoeing. I said that although both can take you over rough patches, the secret to success is knowing how to spot the rapids ahead. With our family, there were rough spots—times when I didn't know if the children would be okay and times when I wanted to give up. They weren't always the most serious problems in the world, but when you're a parent, everything seems serious. Every hurt or scratch, big or small, is painful, not only to your child, but also to you. And yet we all survived. In fact, we not only survived, we thrived. An update on the kids is that all three children are happy, healthy (knock on wood), and gainfully employed. At the time of publication, Jen is 28 and living with her husband in California. She is completing her Ph.D. from Harvard in Jewish studies. Sarah is 26 and finishing her Ph.D. from Duke University in neurobiology. Josh graduated from New York University and is now 24 and working as a sound engineer in New York City.

I tell you all this to reassure you that it is possible to survive and come out the other side of parenting gifted children. My husband and I certainly made mistakes, and yet our children grew into bright, well-adjusted, caring people. In all likelihood, your children will, too. It is in the nature of parenting to make mistakes, but as long as you follow what I like to call the three guiding principles, you and your children should be okay. I'll repeat the three guiding principles from the beginning of the book:

> 1. *Surround your child with unconditional love and a secure environment.*
> 2. *Respect the uniqueness that is within each child.*
> 3. *Identify and nurture your child's talents.*

Now that you've read the whole book, perhaps you can see how important these rules are and how they are evident in each of the 10 issues I discussed about gifted children. Each chapter exemplified some social-emotional issue, and these guiding rules apply to all of them.

Chapter 1 – When Sarah almost shut down due to perfectionism, we reassured her that we would love and respect her no matter what (Rules 1 and 2).

Chapter 2 – When Josh underachieved, we helped him to identify and nurture a talent (Rule 3).

Chapter 3 – When Jen was afraid, we surrounded her with a secure environment (Rule 1).

Chapter 4 – When Sarah was defiant of authority, wanting to stay out late and party, we respected her uniqueness and attempted to shape the defiance into something positive without crushing her spirit (Rule 2). In addition, setting boundaries is part of establishing a loving and secure environment (Rule 1).

Chapter 5 – When Jen was not socially outgoing, we respected her uniqueness and were able to accept that she did not need zillions of friends (Rule 2).

Chapter 6 – When my students constantly questioned me, I was able to take that as a healthy sign, identifying areas of interest and nurturing them (Rule 3).

Chapter 7 – When Josh found something that he loved, we didn't punish him by taking it away. Instead, we attempted to help him become better at it (Rule 3).

Chapter 8 – When Jen fell in love with many different interests, we were able to guide her to see her strengths (Rule 3) and help her finally settle on one area of passion, which she still loves today. We accepted her final choice (Rule 2).

Chapter 9 – When Sarah wanted to quit the spelling bee, we encouraged her to continue to develop her talents (Rule 3) while reassuring her that we would love her no matter what (Rule 1).

Chapter 10 – When Josh developed an interest in creative pursuits, we nurtured that ability (Rule 3), respecting that he was different from his sisters academically (Rule 2).

I also mentioned at the beginning of the book how important it is to trust your instincts. Many of us have good instincts, but we don't always trust them. We need to listen to our small inner voices that say, "Do this—you're the parent." Or, if you don't have good instincts, select a role model—someone who has been through the child-rearing years and whose children are now thriving adults. Talk with this person, not only to solicit advice about particular circumstances, but also about how to relax and enjoy your child. I wonder sometimes about the lack of instincts or the ability to trust them in today's generation of parents. Perhaps it's because we've misinterpreted the advice of experts who seem to suggest that children are extremely fragile. Although it is certainly true that some children are fragile, most children are more resilient than we give them credit for. And if we accept the idea that children are resilient, maybe we can all relax.

I love to watch the television show *Mad Men*, a drama about advertising executives and their families living in the 1960s. I smile as I watch the moms and dads on this show turn to their children, who approach them with issues big and small, with the same words: "Go play." In some ways, that period was a simpler time, although, to be sure, the '50s and '60s were not always the idyllic times portrayed by television shows like *Leave It to Beaver* or *Father Knows Best*. Many mothers stayed at home with their children, and their lives were often restricted by family responsibilities. African Americans could not attend the same schools as their white counterparts. Those times were not good for everyone.

I was a child in the 1960s, so it is hard for me to separate my childhood memories from the turbulent times I read about today in the history books. However, there is one thing that I do remember, and that is how parents in the 1960s seem to be more relaxed about their parenting techniques, perhaps because they were confident that their children were resilient. They realized that as long as children understood that they were loved and supported, as long as they provided the boundaries the children needed, those children would develop into happy and functioning members of society. Today the words "Go play" sound a bit callous, don't they? What if the child is hurt? What if he is emotionally distraught? What if his self-esteem is damaged?

Please understand, I'm not suggesting that every parent respond to every child with the words, "Go play." Certainly, some concerns are serious and need to be addressed differently. However, parents in the '60s knew what we sometimes forget—namely that our children's concerns are often transitory in nature, and their severity may be overblown by well-meaning adults who fear that their children are not resilient. Hovering may occur, which in turn may cause the child to ratchet up the level of demand for more attention. After all, the squeaky wheel gets the grease, doesn't it? It is the wise parent who can learn to differentiate between more serious and less serious concerns, and it is the happy parent who can relax and enjoy the whole child during these fleeting, precious years of youth.

So to add to the three guiding principles, I'm going to suggest a fourth: Don't set up roadblocks by thinking that things are more serious than they are. Trust your parenting instincts, and allow yourself to learn from your experiences with your children. Love your children, and accept them for who they are. Help them be the best that they can be, and the rapids you encounter will turn into mostly smooth canoeing all the way through.

Resources

Introduction

Organizations Dedicated to Gifted Children

Center for Talent Development: www.ctd.northwestern.edu

Center for Talented Youth (CTY): http://cty.jhu.edu

Council for Exceptional Children (CEC): www.cec.sped.org/am/template.cfm?section=Home

Duke Talent Identification Program (TIP): www.tip.duke.edu

National Association for Gifted Children (NAGC): www.nagc.org

National Research Center on the Gifted and Talented (NRC/GT): www.gifted.uconn.edu/nrcgt

Supporting Emotional Needs of the Gifted (SENG): www.sengifted.org

Characteristics of Gifted Children

Books

Sternberg, R., & Reis, S. M. (Eds.). (2004). *Definitions and conceptions of giftedness.* Thousand Oaks, CA: Corwin Press.

Winner, E. (1997). *Gifted children: Myths and realities.* New York: Basic Books.

Articles

Foster, J. (n.d.). *Is my child gifted?* Retrieved from www.sengifted.org/articles_learning/is_my_child_gifted.shtml

Gentry, M., & Kettle, K. (1998). *Distinguishing myths from realities.* Retrieved from www.gifted.uconn.edu/nrcgt/newsletter/winter98/wintr983.html

Hoagies' Gifted Education. (2010). *Characteristics of the gifted child.* Retrieved from www.hoagiesgifted.org/characteristics.htm

National Association for Gifted Children. (2008). *Common gifted education myths.* Retrieved from www.nagc.org/commonmyths.aspx

National Association for Gifted Children. (n.d.). *What is giftedness?* Retrieved from www.nagc.org/index.aspx?id=574&ir

Tolan, S. (1995). *Is it a cheetah?* Retrieved from www.stephanietolan.com/is_it_a_cheetah.htm

Parenting Gifted Children
Books

Clark, B. (2007). *Growing up gifted: Developing the potential of children at home and at school* (7th ed.). New York: Prentice Hall.

Davis, J. L. (2010). *Bright, talented, and Black: A guide for families of African American gifted learners.* Scottsdale, AZ: Great Potential Press.

Delisle, J. R. (2006). *Parenting gifted kids: Tips for raising happy and successful children.* Waco, TX: Prufrock.

Faber, A., & Mazlish, E. (1999). *How to talk so kids will listen and listen so kids will talk.* New York: Avon.

Galbraith, J., & Delisle, J. (1996). *Gifted kids' survival guide.* Minneapolis, MN: Free Spirit.

Isaacson, K. L. J. (2002). *Raisin' brains: Surviving my smart family.* Scottsdale, AZ: Great Potential Press.

Isaacson, K. L. J. (2007). *Life in the fast brain.* Scottsdale, AZ: Great Potential Press.

Kerr, B. A. (1997). *Smart girls: A new psychology of girls, women, and giftedness.* Scottsdale, AZ: Great Potential Press.

Kerr, B. A., & Cohn, S. J. (2001). *Smart boys: Talent, manhood, and the search for meaning.* Scottsdale, AZ: Great Potential Press.

Rimm, S. B. (2007) *How to parent so children will learn.* Scottsdale, AZ: Great Potential Press.

Rimm, S. B. (2007). *Keys to parenting the gifted child* (3rd ed.). Scottsdale, AZ: Great Potential Press.

Rivero, L. (2010). *A parent's guide to gifted teens: Living with intense and creative adolescents.* Scottsdale, AZ: Great Potential Press.

Smutny, J. F. (1991). *Your gifted child: How to recognize and develop the special talents of your child from birth to age seven.* New York: Ballantine.

Walker, S. (2000). *The survival guide for parents of gifted kids: How to understand, live with, and stick up for your gifted child* (Rev. ed.). Minneapolis, MN: Free Spirit.

Webb, J. T., Gore, J. L, Amend, E. R., & DeVries, A. R. (2007). *A parent's guide to gifted children.* Scottsdale, AZ: Great Potential Press.

Articles

Hesslein, J. (2010). *What your kids want you to know.* Retrieved from www.sengifted.org/articles_parenting/hesslein_what_your_kids_want_you_to_know.shtml

Robinson, N. (1993). *Parenting the very young gifted child.* Retrieved from www.gifted.uconn.edu/nrcgt/reports/rbdm9308/rbdm9308.pdf

Silverman, L. K. (1992). *How parents can support gifted children.* Retrieved from www.kidsource.com/kidsource/content/parents.gifted.html

Audio CDs

The NAGC Mile Marker Series. (2010). More information at www.nagc.org/NAGCMileMarker.aspx

Social-Emotional Issues of Gifted Children
Books

Delisle, J., & Galbraith, J. (2002). *When gifted kids don't have all the answers: How to meet their social and emotional needs.* Minneapolis, MN: Free Spirit.

Neihart, M., Reis, S. M., Robinson, N. M., & Moon, S. M. (Eds.). (2002). *The social and emotional development of gifted children: What do we know?* Waco, TX: Prufrock.

Articles

Cross, T. L. (2003). *Social-emotional issues.* Retrieved from www.sengifted.org/articles_social/Cross_CompetingWithMyths AboutTheSocialAndEmotionalDevelopment.shtml

National Association for Gifted Children. (2008). *Peer relationships/social skills/bullies.* Retrieved from www.nagc.org/index.aspx?id=1212

Reis, S. M. (2002). *Social-emotional issues faced by girls in elementary and secondary school.* Retrieved from www.sengifted.org/articles_social/ Reis_SocialAndEmotionalIssuesFacedByGiftedGirls.shtml

Roeper, A. (2005). *The emotional needs of the gifted child.* Retrieved from www.sengifted.org/articles_social/Roeper_TheEmotional NeedsOfTheGiftedChild.shtml

Webb, J. T. (1994). *Nurturing social-emotional development of gifted children.* Retrieved from www.kidsource.com/kidsource/content2/ social_development_gifted.html

Website
Supporting Emotional Needs of the Gifted: www.sengifted.org/articles_ social/index.shtml

Advocacy
Books
Davidson, J., Davison, B., & Vanderkam, L. (2004). *Genius denied: How to stop wasting our brightest young minds.* New York: Simon & Schuster.

Gilman, B. J. (2008). *Academic advocacy for gifted children: A parent's complete guide.* Scottsdale, AZ: Great Potential Press.

Smutny, J. F. (2001). *Stand up for your gifted child: How to make the most of kids' strengths at school and at home.* Minneapolis, MN: Free Spirit.

Articles
National Association for Gifted Children. (2008). *Advocacy toolkit.* Retrieved from www.nagc.org/toolkit.aspx

Movies for Gifted Children and Adults
Bainbridge, C. (2010). *Top 10 movies gifted kids will love.* Retrieved from http://giftedkids.about.com/od/nurturinggiftsandtalents/tp/ gifted_movies.htm

Hébert, T. (2005). Fostering the emotional and social development of gifted children through guided viewing of film. *Roeper Review, 25*(1), 17-21. Retrieved from http://giftedkids.about.com/od/nurturing giftsandtalents/tp/gifted_movies.htm

Hoagies' Gifted Education. (2010). *Movies featuring gifted kids (and adults).* Retrieved from www.hoagiesgifted.org/movies.htm

Chapter 1

Types of Learners (Mastery, Performance)
Books

Dweck, C. (2006). *Mindset: The new psychology of success.* New York: Random House.

Perfectionism
Books

Adderholdt-Elliot, M., & Goldberg, J. (1999). *Perfectionism: What's bad about being too good?* Minneapolis, MN: Free Spirit.

Addleson, J. L., & Wilson, H. (2009). *Letting go of perfect: Overcoming perfectionism in kids.* Waco, TX: Prufrock.

Greenspon, T. (2002). *Freeing our families from perfectionism.* Minneapolis, MN: Free Spirit.

Quindlen, A. (2005). *Being perfect.* New York: Random House.

Articles

Delisle, J. (2003). *Risk-taking and risk-making: Understanding when less than perfection is more than acceptable.* Retrieved from www.sengifted.org/articles_social/Delisle_RisktakingAnd Riskmaking.shtml

Silverman, L. K. (1999). *Perfectionism: The crucible of giftedness.* Retrieved from http://nmgifted.org/GAC%20Resources/Perfectionism%20 The%20Crucible%20of%20Giftedness-SILVERMAN.pdf

Overcoming Failure
Books

Goertzel, V., Goertzel, M. G., Goertzel, T. G., & Hansen, A. M. W. (2004). *Cradles of eminence: Childhoods of more than 700 famous men and women.* Scottsdale, AZ: Great Potential Press.

Chapters 2 & 7

Underachievement and Selective Achievement (and Fostering Interest)
Programs, Clubs, and Academic Competitions

Future Problem Solvers: www.fpspi.org

Odyssey of the Mind: www.odysseyofthemind.com

Oracle ThinkQuest: www.thinkquest.org/en

Summer Institute for the Gifted: www.giftedstudy.org

Books

Karnes, F. A., & Riley, T. L. (2005). *Competitions for talented kids.* Waco, TX: Prufrock.

Rimm, S. (1990). *Underachievement syndrome: Causes and cures.* New York: Apple.

Rimm, S. (2008). *Why bright kids get poor grades and what you can do about it.* Scottsdale, AZ: Great Potential Press.

Rogers, K. B. (2002). *Reforming gifted education: Matching the program to the child.* Scottsdale, AZ: Great Potential Press.

Strip, C. A., & Hirsch, G. (2000). *Helping gifted children soar: A practical guide for parents and teachers.* Scottsdale, AZ: Great Potential Press.

Webb, J. T., Amend, E. R., Webb, N. E., Goerss, J., Beljan, P., & Olenchak, F. R. (2005). *Misdiagnosis and dual diagnoses of gifted children and adults: ADHD, bipolar, OCD, Asperger's, depression, and other disorders.* Scottsdale, AZ: Great Potential Press.

Whitney, C. S., & Hirsch, G. (2007). *A love for learning: Motivation and the gifted child.* Scottsdale, AZ: Great Potential Press.

Articles

Balzac, S. R. (2009). *Maintaining motivation: It's a marathon!* Retrieved from http://sengifted.org/articles_social/balzac_maintaining_motivation.shtml

Baum, S. M., Renzulli, J. S., & Hébert, T. (1995). *The prism metaphor: A new paradigm for reversing underachievement* (CRS95310). Storrs, CT: National Research Center on the Gifted and Talented, University of Connecticut. Retrieved from www.gifted.uconn.edu/nrcgt/baumrenz.html

Delisle, J., & Berger, S. (1990). *Underachieving gifted students.* Retrieved from www.kidsource.com/kidsource/content/underachieving_gifted.html

Hoagies' Gifted Education. (n.d.). *Mentors for gifted children.* Retrieved from www.hoagiesgifted.org/mentors.htm

National Association for Gifted Children. (2008). *Summer programs for gifted students.* Retrieved from www.nagc.org/index.aspx?id=1103

Webb, J. T. (2001). Tips for selecting the right counselor or therapist for your gifted child. *SENG Newsletter, 1*(2), 3-8. Retrieved from www.sengifted.org/articles_parenting/ Webb_TipsFor SelectingTheRightCounselor ForYourGiftedChild.shtml

Pamphlet

Ford, D. Y. (1996). *Reversing underachievement among gifted Black students. Promising practices and programs.* New York: Teachers College Press.

Chapter 3

Sensitivities and Overexcitabilities

Books

American Girl. (2002). *A smart girl's guide to surviving tricky, sticky, icky situations.* Middletown, WI: Pleasant.

Aron, E. (1997). *The highly sensitive person.* New York: Broadway Books.

Dabrowski, K. (1964). *Positive disintegration.* Boston: Little Brown & Co.

Daniels, S., & Piechowski, M. (Eds.). (2009). *Living with intensity: Understanding the sensitivity, excitability, and emotional development of gifted children, adolescents, and adults.* Scottsdale, AZ: Great Potential Press.

Articles

Berger, S. (n.d.). *Gifted children and sensitivity.* Retrieved from http:// school.familyeducation.com/gifted-education/social-skills/38658. html

Comallie-Caplan, L. (2010). *Gifted intensities: Liability or asset.* www. sengifted.org/SMPG/smpg_may10_column.shtml

Comallie-Caplan, L. (2010). *He who laughs last, lasts! Helping your gifted child cope with stress.* Retrieved from www.sengifted.org/SMPG/ smpg_september10_column.shtml

Goerss, J. (2005). *Asynchronous development.* Retrieved from www.sengifted.org/articles_directorscorner/Goerss_Aug05.shtml

Lind, S. (2001). Overexcitability and the gifted. *SENG Newsletter, 1*(1), 3-6. Retrieved from www.sengifted.org/articles_social/Lind_ OverexcitabilityAndTheGifted.shtml

O'Brien, D. (n.d.). *How can I help my child deal with terror?* Retrieved from www.giftedresourcecouncil.org/articles/dealwith.htm

Tolan, S. (1999). *Dabrowski's overexcitabilities: A layman's explanation.* Retrieved from www.stephanietolan.com/dabrowskis.htm

Chapter 4

Communication with Gifted Children
Books

Kurcinka, M. S. (1992). *Raising your spirited child.* New York: Harper Collins.

Articles

O'Brien, D. (n.d.). *How should we communicate with our child?* Retrieved from www.giftedresourcecouncil.org/articles/communicate.htm

Probst, B. (2005). Managing life with a challenging child: What to do when your gifted but difficult child is driving you crazy. *Twice Exceptional Newsletter, 10.* Retrieved from www.sengifted.org/articles_parenting/Probst_ManagingLifeWithAChallengingChild.html

Chapter 5

Social Issues
Books

Duke, M. P., Nowicki. S., & Martin, E. A. (1996). *Teaching your child the language of social success.* Atlanta, GA: Peachtree.

Frankel, F. (1996). *Good friends are hard to find: Help your child find, make and keep friends.* Los Angeles: Perspective.

Articles

Bainbridge, C. (n.d.). *If introverts ran the world.* Retrieved from http://giftedkids.about.com/u/ua/glossary/introverted_world.htm

Burruss, J. D., & Kaenzig, L. (1999). Introversion: The often-forgotten factor impacting the gifted. *Virginia Association for the Gifted Newsletter, 21*(1). Retrieved from www.sengifted.org/articles_social/BurrussKaenzig_IntroversionTheOftenForgotten.shtml

Gross, M. U. M. (2002, May). "Play partner" or "sure shelter": What gifted children look for in friendship. *SENG Newsletter*, 1-3. Retrieved from www.sengifted.org/articles_social/Gross_PlayPartnerOrSureShelter.shtml

Lind, S. (2004). *Tips for parents of introverts*. Retrieved from www.sengifted.org/articles_parenting/Lind_TipsForParents Introverts.shtml

Rimm, S. (1988). Popularity ends at grade twelve. *Gifted Child Today, 11*, 42-44.

Schuler, P. A. (2002). Teasing and gifted children. *SENG Newsletter, 2*(1), 3-4. Retrieved from www.sengifted.org/articles_social/Schuler_TeasingAndGiftedChildren.shtml

Chapter 6

Dealing with the Need to Know
Articles

American Association of School Librarians, & Association for Educational Communications. (1998). *Information literacy standards for student learning*. Retrieved from www.ala.org/ala/mgrps/divs/aasl/aaslarchive/pubsarchive/informationpower/InformationLiteracyStandards_final.pdf

Bainbridge, C. (n.d.). *Dealing with never-ending questions*. Retrieved from http://giftedkids.about.com/od/nurturinggiftsandtalents/qt/questions.htm

Olszewski-Kubilius, P. (n.d.). *Is your school using best practices for instruction?* Retrieved from www.ctd.northwestern.edu/resources/topics/displayArticle/?id=313

Schneider, J. (2009). Besides Google: Guiding gifted elementary students onto the entrance ramp of the information superhighway. *Gifted Child Today, 32*(1), 27-31.

Schrock, K. (n.d.). *Teacher helpers: Critical evaluation information*. Retrieved from http://school.discoveryeducation.com/schrockguide/eval.html

Squirrelnet.com Tutorials and Guides. (n.d.). Retrieved from www.squirrelnet.com/TutorialsAndGuides/start.asp

University of Wisconsin-Madison. (2004). *Checklist for evaluating websites.* Retrieved from http://steenbock.library.wisc.edu/instruct/
ChecklistEvalWeb11132007-1.pdf

Chapter 7

(See Chapters 2 & 7)

Chapter 8

Career Guidance and Multipotentiality
Books

Berger, S. (2006). *College planning for gifted students: Choosing and getting
into the right college.* Waco, TX: Prufrock.

Goldberg, J. (2008). *Careers for geniuses and other gifted types* (2nd ed.).
New York: McGraw Hill.

Articles

Berger, S. (1990). *College planning for gifted and talented youth.* Retrieved
from www.kidsource.com/kidsource/content/college_planning.
html

Kerr, B. (1990). *Career planning for gifted and talented youth.* Retrieved
from www.kidsource.com/kidsource/content/career_planning.html

Kosin, P., & Tierre, W. (n.d.). *Early career planning is essential for gifted
adolescents.* Retrieved from www.ctd.northwestern.edu/resources/
topics/displayArticle/?id=108

Olszewski-Kubilius, P. (n.d.). *Thinking about early entrance to college.*
Retrieved from www.ctd.northwestern.edu/resources/topics/
displayArticle/?id=153

Renzulli Learning. (n.d.). *The Renzulli personal success plan: A tool
for helping youth plan their dreams.* Retrieved from
www.renzullilearningsystems.com/downloads/PSP_Helping_
Youth_Plan_Their_Dreams.doc

Website

Bureau of Labor and Statistics. (2011). *Occupational outlook handbook.*
Retrieved from www.bls.gov/oco

Chapter 9

Persistence and Dealing with Failure

Books

Magruder, T., Pavette, S., Watkins, M., & Haley, A. (Eds.). (2003). *True stories: Girls' inspiring stories of courage and heart*. Middletown, WI: Pleasant.

National Geographic Society. *World history biographies* (series). Available at http://shop.nationalgeographic.com/ngs/category/world-history-biographies?categoryId=S010

Odean, K. (2002). *Great books for girls: More than 600 books to inspire today's girls and tomorrow's women*. New York: Random House.

Articles

Clark, L. (2001). *Helping children achieve success and learn from failure*. Retrieved from http://ohioline.osu.edu/flm01/pdf/FS14.pdf

Great Schools Staff. (n.d.). *Teaching young kids persistence*. Retrieved from www.greatschools.org/students/academic-skills/teaching-persistence-1st-and-2nd-grade.gs?content=2429

Tyson, X. (2005). *Teaching children persistence*. Retrieved from http://mabryonline.org/blogs/tyson/archive/2005/09/teaching_children_persistence.html

Chapter 10

Creativity

Books

Amabile, T. (1989). *Growing up: Nurturing a lifetime of creativity*. Norwalk, CT: Crown.

Esquivel, G. B., & Houtz, J. C. (Eds.). (2000). *Creativity and giftedness in culturally diverse students*. Cresskill, NJ: Hampton.

Osborne, A. F. (1993). *Applied imagination: Principles and procedures of creative problem solving* (3rd ed.). Amherst, MA: Creative Education Foundation Press.

Piirto, J. (2004). *Understanding creativity*. Scottsdale, AZ: Great Potential Press.

Pink, D. (2006). *A whole new mind: Why right-brainers will rule the world*. New York: Berkley Publishing Group.

Robinson, K. (2001). *Out of our minds: Learning to be creative.* Oxford, UK: Capstone.

Smutny, J. (Ed.). (1998). *The young gifted child: Potential and promise, an anthology.* New York: Hampton Press.

Treffinger, D. J. (1993). Stimulating creativity: Issues and future directions. In S. G. Isaksen, M. C. Murdock, R. L. Firestien, & D. J. Treffinger (Eds.), *Nurturing and developing creativity: The emergence of a discipline* (pp. 8-27). Norwood, NJ: Ablex.

Articles

Louisiana gumbo: Understanding creativity. (n.d.). Retrieved from www.ctd.northwestern.edu/resources/topics/displayArticle/?id=127

Torrance, E. P., & Goff, K. (1990). *Fostering academic creativity in gifted students.* Retrieved from www.kidsource.com/kidsource/content/academic_creativity.html

Endnotes

1   Neihart, Reis, Robinson, & Moon, 2002
2   Maslow & Lowery, 1998
3   Bowlby, 1969
4   Rogers & Silverman, 1997
5   Joseph, 1999
6   Blair, 2002
7   Greenberg, 1999
8   Maslow, 1943
9   Bandura, 1977
10 Dweck, 2007
11 Renzulli, 1978
12 Kaufmann, 1980, p. 73
13 Ames, 1992
14 Hollingworth, 1926
15 Maslow, 1970
16 Burns, 1980
17 Hamachek, 1978
18 Schuler, 1999
19 Reivich, & Shatté, 2002
20 Webb, Gore, Amend, & DeVries, 2007
21 Renzulli & Reis, 1994
22 Davis & Rimm, 2004, p. 306
23 Reis & McCoach, 2000
24 Rimm, 1986; Whitney & Hirsch, 2007
25 Siegle & McCoach, 2005
26 Siegle & McCoach, 2005

27   Dabrowski, 1964; see also Daniels & Piechowski, 2009
28   Silverman, 1997
29   Webb et al., 2005
30   Webb, 2001
31   Silverman, 1983
32   Osborne, 1993
33   Bain & Bell, 2004
34   Rimm, 2002
35   Bain & Bell, 2004
36   Luftig & Nichols, 1990
37   Luftig & Nichols, 1990
38   Davis & Rimm, 2004
39   Hollingworth, 1926
40   Gross, 2002
41   Silverman, 1993
42   Rimm, 1988
43   Sword, 2002
44   Dabrowski, 1964
45   Bainbridge, 2010
46   McGuinan, 2011
47   American Association of School Librarians & Association for Educational Communications and Technology, 1998
48   Schneider, 2009
49   J. Innes, personal communication, February 4, 2011
50   Leu, 2006
51   J. Innes, personal communication, February 4, 2011
52   Otterman, 2009
53   Bandura & Adams, 1977
54   Fredrickson, 1979, p. 268
55   Achter, Lubinski, & Benbow, 1996
56   Greene, 2005
57   Olszewski-Kubilius, Limburg-Weber, & Pfeiffer, 2003
58   Reis et al., 1993
59   Dweck, 2006
60   Pink, 2006
61   Robinson, 2001
62   Guilford, 1967
63   Amabile, 1989; Treffinger, 1993
64   Osborne, 1993

References

Achter, J. A., Lubinski, D., & Benbow, C. (1996). Multipotentiality among the intellectually gifted: "It was never there and already it's vanishing." *Journal of Counseling Psychology, 43*(1), 65-76.

Amabile, T. (1989). *Growing up: Nurturing a lifetime of creativity.* Norwalk, CT: Crown.

American Association of School Librarians, & Association for Educational Communications and Technology. (1998). *Information literacy standards for student learning.* Chicago: American Library Association.

Ames, C. (1992). Classrooms: Goals, structures, and motivations. *Journal of Educational Psychology, 84*(3), 261-271.

Bain, S. K., & Bell, S. M. (2004). Social self-concept, social attributions, and peer relationships in fourth, fifth, and sixth graders. *Gifted Child Quarterly, 48*, 167-178.

Bainbridge, C. (2010). *Dealing with never-ending questions.* Retrieved from http://giftedkids.about.com/od/nurturinggiftsandtalents/qt/questions.htm

Bandura, A. (1977). Self-efficacy: Toward a unifying theory of behavioral change. *Psychological Review, 84*, 191-215.

Bandura, A., & Adams, N. E. (1977). Analysis of self-efficacy theory of behavioral change. *Cognitive Therapy and Research, 1*(4), 287-310.

Blair, C. (2002). School readiness: Integrating cognition and emotion in a neurobiological conceptualization of children's functioning at school entry. *American Psychologist, 57*, 111-127.

Bowlby, J. (1969). *Attachment and loss: Vol. 1. Attachment.* London: Hogarth Press & the Institute of Psycho-Analysis.

Burns, D. D. (1980, November). The perfectionist's script for self-defeat. *Psychology Today,* 70-76.

Dabrowski, K. (1964). *Positive disintegration.* London: Little, Brown & Co.

Daniels, S., & Piechowski, M. (Eds.). (2009). *Living with intensity: Understanding the sensitivity, excitability, and emotional development of gifted children, adolescents, and adults.* Scottsdale, AZ: Great Potential Press.

Davis, G. A., & Rimm, S. B. (2004). *Education of the gifted and talented* (5th ed.). Boston: Pearson.

Dweck, C. (2006). *Mindset: The new psychology of success.* New York: Random House.

Dweck, C. (2007). Is math a gift? Beliefs that put females at risk. In S. J. Ceci & W. M. Williams (Eds.), *Why aren't more women in science?* (pp. 47-55). Washington, DC: American Psychological Association.

Fredrickson, R. H. (1979). Career development and the gifted. In N. Colangelo & R. T. Zaffrann (Eds.), *New voices in counseling the gifted* (pp. 264-276). Dubuque, IA: Kendall/Hunt.

Greenberg, M. (1999). Attachment and psychopathology in childhood. In J. Cassidy & P. Shaver (Eds.), *Handbook of attachment: Theory, research and clinical applications* (pp. 469-496). New York: Guilford.

Greene, M. (2005). Multipotentiality: Issues and considerations for career planning. *Duke Gifted Letter, 6*(1), 13. Retrieved from www.dukegiftedletter.com/articles/vol6no1_feature.html

Gross, M. U. M. (2002). Musings: Gifted children and the gifted of friendship. *Understanding Our Gifted, 14*(3), 27-29.

Guilford, J. P. (1967). Creative abilities in the arts. *Psychological Review, 64*(2), 110-118.

Hamachek, D. E. (1978). Psychodynamics of normal and neurotic perfectionism. *Psychology, 15,* 27-33.

Hollingworth, L. S. (1926). *Gifted children: Their nature and nurture.* New York: Macmillan.

Joseph, R. (1999). Environmental influences on neural plasticity, the limbic system, emotional development and attachment: A review. *Child Psychiatry and Human Development, 29,* 189-208.

Kaufmann, F. A. (1980). *A follow-up study of the 1964-1968 Presidential Scholars.* [Doctoral dissertation, University of Georgia, 1979]. Dissertation Abstracts International, 40A, 5794A. (University Microfilms No. 80-10, 601).

Leu, D. J. (2006). New literacies, reading research, and the challenges of change: A deictic perspective. In J. V. Hoffman, D. L. Schallert, C. M. Fairbanks, J. Worthy, & B. Maloch (Eds.), *55th Yearbook of the National Reading Conference* (pp. 1-20). Oak Creek, WI: National Reading Conference.

Luftig, R. L., & Nichols, M. L. (1990). Assessing the social status of gifted students by their age peers. *Gifted Child Quarterly, 34,* 111-115.

Maslow, A. H. (1943). A theory of human motivation. *Psychological Review, 50*(4), 370-396.

Maslow, A. H. (1970). *Motivation and personality* (Rev. ed.). New York: Harper & Row.

Maslow, A. H., & Lowery, R. (Eds.). (1998). *Toward a psychology of being* (3rd ed.). New York: Wiley & Sons.

McGuinan, B. (2011). *How big is the internet?* Retrieved from www.wisegeek.com/how-big-is-the-internet.htm

Neihart, M., Reis, S. M., Robinson, N. M., & Moon, S. M. (Eds.). (2002). *The social and emotional development of gifted children: What do we know?* Washington, DC: National Association for Gifted Children.

Olszewski-Kubilius, P., Limburg-Weber, L., & Pfeiffer, S. (2003). *Early gifts: Recognizing and nurturing children's talents.* Waco, TX: Prufrock.

Osborne, A. F. (1993). *Applied imagination: Principles and procedures of creative problem solving* (3rd ed.). Amherst, MA: Creative Education Foundation Press.

Otterman, S. (2009, Nov. 20). Tips for the admissions test...to kindergarten. *The New York Times.* Retrieved from www.newyorktimes.com

Pink, D. (2006). *A whole new mind: Why right-brainers will rule the world.* New York: Berkley Publishing Group.

Reis, S. M., & McCoach, D. B. (2000). The underachievement of gifted students: What do we know and where do we go? *Gifted Child Quarterly, 44*, 152-179.

Reis, S. M., Westberg, K. L., Kulikowich, J., Caillard, F., Hébert, T., Plucker, J., Purcell, J. H., Rogers, J. B., & Smist, J. M. (1993). *Why not let high ability students start school in January? The curriculum compacting study.* (Research Monograph 93106). Storrs, CT: National Research Center on the Gifted and Talented, University of Connecticut.

Reivich, K., & Shatté, A. (2002). *The resilience factor: 7 keys to finding your inner strength and overcoming life's hurdles.* New York: Random House.

Renzulli, J. (1978). What makes giftedness? Reexamining a definition. *Phi Delta Kappan, 60*, 180-184.

Renzulli, J. S., & Reis, S. M. (1994). Research related to the Schoolwide Enrichment Model. *Gifted Child Quarterly, 38*, 2-14.

Rimm, S. (1986). *Underachievement syndrome: Causes and cures.* New York: Apple.

Rimm, S. (1988). Popularity ends at grade twelve. *Gifted Child Today, 11*, 42-44.

Rimm, S. (2002). Peer pressures and social acceptance of gifted students. In M. Neihart, S. M. Reis, N. M. Robinson, & S. M. Moon (Eds.), *The social and emotional development of gifted children: What do we know?* (pp. 13-18). Washington, DC: National Association for Gifted Children.

Robinson, K. (2001). *Out of our minds: Learning to be creative.* Oxford: Capstone.

Rogers, K., & Silverman, L. (1997, Nov.). *Exceptionally and profoundly gifted children.* Paper presented at the National Association for Gifted Children Annual Convention, Little Rock, AR.

Schneider, J. (2009). Besides Google: Guiding gifted elementary students onto the entrance ramp of the information superhighway. *Gifted Child Today, 32*(1), 27-31.

Schuler, P. (1999). *Voices of perfectionism: Perfectionistic gifted adolescents in a rural middle school.* (Research Monograph 99140). Storrs, CT:

The National Research Center on the Gifted and Talented, University of Connecticut.

Siegle, D., & McCoach, D. B. (2005). Making a difference: Motivating gifted students who are not achieving. *Teaching Exceptional Children, 38*(1), 22-27.

Silverman, L. K. (1983). Issues in affective development of the gifted. In J. Van Tassel-Baska (Ed.), *A practical guide for counseling the gifted in a school setting* (pp. 15-30). Reston, VA: Council for Exceptional Children.

Silverman, L. K. (1993). *Counseling the gifted and talented*. Denver, CO: Love.

Silverman, L. K. (1997). The construct of asynchronous development. *Peabody Journal of Education, 72*, 36-58.

Sword, L. (2002). *The gifted introvert*. Retrieved from www.talentdevelop. com/articles/GiftIntrov.html

Treffinger, D. J. (1993). Stimulating creativity: Issues and future directions. In S. G. Isaksen, M. C. Murdock, R. L. Firestien, & D. J. Treffinger (Eds.), *Nurturing and developing creativity: The emergence of a discipline* (pp. 8-27). Norwood, NJ: Ablex.

Webb, J. T. (2001). Tips for selecting the right counselor or therapist for your gifted child. *SENG Newsletter, 1*(2), 3-4, 8.

Webb, J. T., Amend, E. R., Webb, N. E., Goerss, J., Beljan, P., & Olenchak, F. R. (2005). *Misdiagnosis and dual diagnoses of gifted children and adults: ADHD, bipolar, OCD, Asperger's, depression, and other disorders*. Scottsdale, AZ: Great Potential Press.

Webb, J. T., Gore, J. L., Amend, E. R., & DeVries, A. R. (2007). *A parent's guide to gifted children*. Scottsdale, AZ: Great Potential Press.

Whitney, C. S., & Hirsch, G. (2007). *A love for learning: Motivation and the gifted child*. Scottsdale, AZ: Great Potential Press.

Index

About the Author

Nancy Heilbronner, Ph.D., is an Assistant Professor of Instructional Leadership at Western Connecticut State University, where she teaches and advises in doctoral level courses in talent development, creativity, and statistics. She is on the Board of the Connecticut Association for Gifted Children and also serves on committees for the National Association for Gifted Children.

Dr. Heilbronner became interested in gifted and talented education when her own children were identified as gifted. She was a teacher of the gifted for 10 years at both the elementary and middle school levels. She earned her Ph.D. in gifted education from the University of Connecticut, where she worked with leaders in the field. Since then, she has been active in researching and publishing in the field of gifted education. Dr. Heilbronner is the recipient of a number of research grants. Her previous book, ThinkData, co-authored by Drs. Joseph S. Renzulli and Del Siegle, is a guide for teachers of gifted science students. She has also authored numerous

parent and teacher articles on gifted children, gifted education, and science education. In addition, she has lectured and provided dozens of professional development and parenting workshops on these topics throughout the United States.

Dr. Heilbronner has been extremely active in her community, serving as the president of her school's PTA and on other steering committees for not-for-profit organizations. A breast-cancer survivor, she also served on steering committees for local breast cancer fundraising organizations. Additionally, she started a parenting group in her community that focused on parent education and advocacy for gifted children.

Dr. Heilbronner lives with her husband, two cats, and a puppy in rural Connecticut. She is the parent of the three co-authors of the book and is now happily anticipating her first grandchild.